TO DIE IS GAIN

STEPHANIE WESCO

TO DIE IS GAIN

"To Die Is Gain" is property of Stephanie Wesco and is officially trademarked.

Bible quotations are from the King James Version.

Copyright © 2020

stephaniewesco.com

All rights reserved. No part of this publication may be reproduced, stored in a computer for later retrieval, or transmitted by any form or by any means—except for brief quotations, which may be used in advertising or printed reviews. Any exceptions must have prior written permission from the author.

❦ Created with Vellum

FOREWORD

Have you ever met anyone who completely surprised you? I have—it was Stephanie Wesco! Don't get me wrong; my expectations were high going in. By all accounts, this widow of a missionary martyr, who himself registered the highest mark in missionary service in my lifetime, was at the very least an awesome helpmeet to her husband. Surrendering to missionary service in an unstable nation with eight young children makes her Superwoman. I knew that her growing up as a pastor's kid with nine younger siblings meant she was a problem-solver and a leader. I assure you she proved to be all those things and much more. She is a brilliant well-spoken lady with a compassionate soul and a story to tell. And it's not just any story but a piece of Christian history that will be shared for generations.

I met Stephanie when she was going through terrible trials. She knew all too well the darkness and misery associated with great hurt and disappointment. She witnessed the murder of her dear husband. Then with the help of great Christians, she escaped a volatile situation to safety with eight kids in tow. Her trials, though horrific, were filled with testimonies of her Savior. Her relationship with the Lord is in no way symbolic or for show—it is real, a living daily walk with the Creator of the universe. She practices what I've preached for years.

Foreword

The world we live in encourages people to design an image that is polished, perfected and presented to one's social media's filter of choice. For people going through trials, there's no special Facebook status to indicate a person's inner turmoil, and the darkest of their thoughts are deemed inappropriate for our consumption. I have shared in Stephanie's inner thoughts and find her to be godly, humble and worthy of His trust. She is a help to those struggling in darkness. Her life shares the Lord's grace.

I have witnessed her spirit of love as she forgave not only her husband's murderers but also a group of disingenuous people bent on controlling or hurting her. Many times, I heard her cry as she shared Joseph-like stories with me. I have shared in her anger and with her begged our Lord for clear leading and forgiveness. I have witnessed firsthand in her life the results of the Lord's promises to care for widows. Then to my amazement I watched her ask the Lord to help her forgive the petty and those trying to hurt her. The Lord has used her example to edify my being and to help me become a better man.

Like Job before her, she trusts the biblical principle that the Lord is close to the brokenhearted and saves those with a contrite spirit. This book is filled with examples of obstacles and mountains to climb—many too great for any person to conquer—yet with the Lord out front she scales each one. Though I am very familiar with her story and have read it several times, I cannot put this book down. Her captivating writing has us standing next to Charles and her throughout their lives.

My prayer is that you, like me, will come away from reading this book with a closer relationship with the Lord.

For Christ and His Church,
Doug Carragher, Th.D.
Author of *Wounded Spirits—A Biblical Approach to PTSD*

DEDICATION

This book is dedicated to the memory of the man I loved with all my heart, Charles (this is our testimony of Christ's love) and to my eight precious children for their love, patience, and understanding of my ups and downs through the process of writing this book. Their prayers, words of encouragement, and hugs have often helped me move forward when I wanted to quit.

ACKNOWLEDGMENTS

"My soul doth magnify the Lord, and my spirit hath rejoiced in God my Savior" (Luke 1:46–47).

Thank you to my precious Savior. Without His love, grace, peace, and light for my path in the darkest hours of life, I would be lost and hopeless. He alone is worthy! He is more real and treasured to me than ever before.

I am so grateful for my parents and their unwavering love, support, encouragement, and belief in God's eternal plan and purpose in all He has allowed in my life. Their willingness to sacrifice their time and energy to help with watching the children while I worked means more to me than words can say.

Steve and Rhonda Hicks and their family were some of our best friends long before Charles' death, but since then they have proven themselves many times over. They exemplify sacrificial love, compassion, and the heart of Christ! Without them and their help and support, this book would not have become a reality.

Thank you to Pastor Frank McClure and his wife Gwen for opening their beautiful guest apartment to me on several occasions. The majority of this book was written within their walls and because of their hospitality.

I will always thank the Lord for giving us the Sinclair family as friends and co-laborers. Even though our initial plans of working together in Cameroon were completely shattered, we continue "striving together for the faith of the gospel" (Philippians 1:27).

To each one who has lifted the children and me up before the throne of grace, your prayers have been life support for us. Your cries to God on our behalf have contributed greatly to the writing of this book!

Doug and Debbie Carragher became two of my greatest encouragers, friends, and confidants in early 2019. Because of their support, trustworthiness, and constant giving of hope, my journey of healing finally began to happen. Working on this book together has led to laughter and tears. They daily remind me that God heard my desperate heart cries for help and hope and that He loves and cares for my children and me (Proverbs 13:20).

ABOUT THE AUTHOR

Stephanie Wesco was born and raised in a pastor's home, married to a preacher, and spent many years involved in serving the Lord as a pastor's/missionary's wife. She is mother to eight beautiful children, and understands what life looks like, balancing raising and teaching little ones, while being actively involved in multiple realms of local church ministry. During those years, God allowed many trials in her life, which He used to draw her closer to Him, as she often struggled to see His purposes in the midst of emotional trauma.

During their three years of deputation, while preparing to go to Cameroon, West Africa, Stephanie and her family learned what living constantly on the road felt like. Through the multiple physical trials God allowed in her life during those years, Stephanie learned to trust in and depend on the Lord for grace and strength to live every moment of every day. Witnessing her husband, Charles Wesco, be martyred in front of her in Cameroon, was indeed the hardest trial of her faith, bringing with it changes to every realm of life, and the traumatic effects of PTSD. God would become real to her, like never before in the coming months, as she found His Word her chief and often only comfort, and then began to find healing through PTSD counseling sessions with Doug and Debbie Carragher.

As she has found her Savior and His promises true, Stephanie has also found His heart of love filling her to help others who are in need of healing from trauma, abuse, and multiple symptoms of PTSD. As a certified counselor with Wounded Spirits' PTSD ministry, she now spends much of her time reaching out and ministering to many ladies in need of hope and encouragement, along with teaching and one-on-one counseling with ladies/children at PTSD workshops and camps. In recent months, after being involved in writing/composing what she loves to call, "songs in the night," Stephanie and her children have produced their first sacred music album, "Steadfast in Trials." Steadfast in Trials is available at all media outlets. She currently resides in the midwestern United States with her eight children.

PREFACE

Before the beginning of time, God had a perfect plan for a very special man. He planned his parents, his time of birth, his childhood, his profession, his calling, his wife, his children, his ministry, his purpose for living. So much would transpire to bring about God's ultimate purpose for that man's life—to live and die for his Savior. That man was my husband, and this is his story—and mine.

TABLE OF CONTENTS

Chapter 1, A Blessed Life
    Chapter 2, To Live Is Christ
    Chapter 3, Our Challenging Courtship
    Chapter 4, Our Heaven on Earth
    Chapter 5, Broken
    Chapter 6, The Call To The Harvest
    Chapter 7, Finding God Faithful
    Chapter 8, "We're Home!"
    Chapter 9, To Die Is Gain
    Chapter 10, "Where's Daddy?"
    Chapter 11, Living In Shock
    Chapter 12, "Why Am I Here?"
    Chapter 13, Drowning
    Chapter 14, Completely Broken
    Chapter 15, Regrouping

Appendix A, Charles' Sermon Notes
    Appendix B, Charles' Quotes
    Appendix C, Charles' Spiritual Preparation

1
A BLESSED LIFE

Late on the night of May 7, 1985, I arrived—my parents' firstborn! They had married in June the year before, and my father was in the middle of Bible college. From the time of my birth, my parents dedicated me to the Lord and began raising me to be committed, even as a child, to serving Him. Some of my first memories are of my parents singing with me. I also remember my aunts and uncles, our family devotions, and lots of Bible memory. Over the years the Lord blessed me with nine amazing sisters and brothers, the youngest of whom was born a few months after I got married! My mom willingly and lovingly poured herself into homeschooling all of us, devoting her time and energy to every aspect of our education. Both my parents instilled in me a love for reading and studying as well as for music. As a child, I was constantly made aware of my need for a Savior from my sin.

Dad, Mom and me - age 10 months

One evening while Dad was reading to us during family devotions, my little heart was suddenly struck with the reality that I was a sinner who was going to die and go to hell unless I accepted Jesus as my Savior from sin. I was so scared! I will never forget my dad looking up, seeing the expression of fear on my face, and asking me what was wrong. I told him that I knew I was a sinner and would go to hell if I died. I'll be forever grateful for the love my dad showed me as he took me to my bedroom and carefully went through the salvation verses that I had already memorized, thanks to my parents' diligence. I will always remember kneeling there with him by the bed and asking Jesus to forgive my sin and come into my heart to save me. Even as a child, I knew I was a sinner. I was very aware I had sinned and fallen short of God's glory and could not save myself. I knew "the wages of sin is death; but the gift of God is eternal life" (Romans 3:23). This was the reason I was so troubled that evening. The reality of my sin separating me from God became so clear in my heart, and I knew that in order for that separation to be removed, I had to accept God's gift of salvation. I knew He loved me. One of the very first verses my parents had taught me was, "For God so loved the world, that he gave his only begotten Son, that whosoever believeth in him should not perish, but have everlasting life" (John 3:16). All God asked of me was to seek His forgiveness for my sin and place my childlike faith in Him for His salvation! When I did that, I became His child!

A few years later, I found myself seriously doubting my salvation. So, as a ten-year-old, I prayed again, asking God to save me. Looking back, I believe I was saved the first time, but the second time was, at the very least a big step of surrendering my life and will to God. I was baptized at the age of thirteen as a public step of obedience to the Lord.

Me - 4 years old

My dad was my pastor throughout my growing-up years, and I

will always be grateful for his faithfulness to the Word of God, as he preached week after week through many books of the Bible and on many different topics. Through his preaching, he was training me up in the way I should go. My dad's assistant pastor and his wife also had an incredible impact on my life; as did a number of others in our church. So many invested so much in me through their examples of faithfulness, servants' spirits, and lives that displayed what being sold out for God looks like in everyday life.

Sunday school was something I eagerly looked forward to every week as a young child since my aunt and uncle poured themselves into all of us who were in their class! I'll always remember fun song times, the stories my uncle told with his puppets, and the incentives they gave us to learn verses. Every class was another seed of love sown in my heart, for loving others and serving God. They poured into me in ways that I could never thank them enough for.

My mom's parents were dairy farmers, and many childhood summers were spent at their house and on the farm, feeding calves, cleaning out stalls, and having serious playtime with the cousins. My grandma was the best cook and baker in the whole world! Her cakes, cookies, pies, and meals were delicious beyond description, and from the time I was a very little girl, she would let me help her bake in the kitchen. She was an incredible hostess, always making anything she cooked look beautiful. She taught me to have a love for working in the kitchen, baking, decorating cakes, and serving others. Those childhood days are precious memories I will always treasure. Both sets of my grandparents invested in me and passed down to me the precious gift of a godly heritage, for which I am eternally grateful!

Being a big sister was so much fun! When I was nine years old, the Lord gave our family twin baby girls. Hope and Joy were "my" first babies. Though I already had two sisters and a brother, the twins were the first of my siblings that came along after I was old enough to begin to comprehend all that was involved in taking care of babies by watching my mother work so hard to care for not one, but two newborns—not to mention the rest of us! I loved getting to help her by holding and rocking them at night when they were fussy and doing anything else she would let me do to help care for them. Later, when two more baby sisters came along and then a little brother, one of my greatest joys was getting to love on them, read to them, and do things with them.

Doing school, studying, and learning new things were three of my favorite activities. Reading was a passion, and I loved missionary biographies and mystery stories. My goal was always to crack the mystery before the author revealed the answers. Music and history were my absolute favorite subjects, with hours poured into learning to play the piano, flute, clarinet, and accordion. I struggled with math and science through grade school, but when high school came, I fell back in love with those subjects and thoroughly enjoyed business math plus all thing's algebra, geometry, chemistry, and so on. Since I thought that I would end up being a missionary in a Spanish-speaking country someday, I took Spanish throughout high school, learning just enough to get me into trouble! My parents were very focused on our having good Bible classes during our school years, for which I will always be thankful. No matter what, Bible memory and Bible class always happened first every day, and I learned so much about God, His Word, and character throughout those years. When I was a child, Dad spent a lot of time with my siblings and me in family devotions, teaching us Bible doctrines, and drilling us on verses that went along with them.

Me - 6 years old

Our church was part of a ministry that helped produce Scripture portions to send around the world, and during our growing-up years, we spent hours putting them together as a family. Those evenings are some of my greatest memories, as we worked as a team, knowing that we were serving Jesus and doing something eternally important.

My parents did a phenomenal job of being hospitable; our home was constantly open to pastors, evangelists, and missionaries. Those people became my role models, my heroes—people I wanted to emulate. So many of them took time to interact with me, as a young person, and their investment in my life had long-lasting effects on me. I am a living legacy of their love, sacrifice, and mentorship.

As a young teenager, I knew that God was calling me to serve Him, and at the age of fifteen, I went forward at the end of a service and surrendered to serve the Lord. There were still areas of my life, though, that I wanted to hold on to for myself. As a senior in high school, while attending a Bible conference with my dad, I came to the point of complete surrender to whatever His will was for my life, and

I was very certain His will was going to include my being a missionary. The message God used to bring me to that point was on the power of His all-sufficient grace that enables us to do anything He calls us to do. I never dreamed that those words would come to mean more to me sixteen years later than they ever could have when I was seventeen.

I had many aspirations, ideas, hopes, and dreams, not all of which would come to fruition, but looking back, the ones that God had for me were accomplished. As my childhood years came to a close, I never could have dreamed what lay ahead, but I will always be thankful for the wonderful foundation laid by so many people God used, and that played a huge role in the coming years.

High School Graduation - 2003

2

TO LIVE IS CHRIST

Charles Truman Wesco was born August 24, 1974, the oldest of ten children. He was named for both his grandfathers. His father was serving in the US Air Force at the time, so Charles was born at K. I. Sawyer Air Force Base in northern Michigan. Charles had fond memories of his childhood years when his father was pastoring a small Baptist church in western Indiana. He accepted Jesus Christ as his Savior at the age of four and never doubted that God had kept His promise to give him the precious gift of forgiveness from sin and eternal life. As a child, Charles loved listening to his father preach, and it was during one of those services that God impressed on his heart that he needed to obey the Lord and be baptized as a public testimony that he had been born again. He was a little nervous about going forward by himself, though, so he asked his younger brother to go with him. His brother agreed, and the two of them went forward together and were baptized soon after.

Charles took his role as the oldest of the children very seriously and invested thousands of hours, dollars, and prayers in the lives of his siblings, teaching them how to read, to write, and to do many things in other realms of life. It was because of his direct influence on their lives and investment of time helping them with Bible memory that a couple of his little brothers got saved.

As a young child, Charles began making food for his family, and he especially loved baking bread. He was also good at cake-decorating and did an amazing job over and over again on multiple cakes for his parents and siblings. His love for the kitchen and making meals proved a huge blessing after I had babies since he always made sure I had wholesome, healthy food to enjoy during recovery. We made more loaves of bread together than I could even count. We used it as an outreach opportunity during the holidays, often giving bread as gifts to neighbors and other people. In the last several years before we went to Cameroon, Charles taught Daniel and Charles Jr. how to make bread with his own recipe. As I look back on those teaching times when my OCD went crazy because of the insane mess their endeavors together would leave in my kitchen, I smile, thanking the Lord that Charles spent those precious times with his sons.

Charles - around 7 years old

Charles loved learning, especially anything related to the Bible, so he began memorizing Scripture at a young age. His parents encouraged him with the incentive that they would buy him his very own Scofield Study Bible if he memorized an entire book of the Bible. I remember him joking about how, as an eight-year-old, he started researching at the beginning and decided that Genesis, as well as many of the books following, would take way too much time and work. Then he came to the book of Jonah and decided that it was perfect. Since it had only forty verses and was also a story, it was a double win. He memorized the book of Jonah and got his very own study Bible. He never would have dreamed that many years later God would use his memorizing of that book to minister to hundreds and hundreds of adults and children across America and Africa.

Throughout his growing-up years, Charles was an avid reader and loved to study. He kept timesheets to hold himself accountable and even before the age of twelve had developed hard-core character qualities of determination and diligence in everything he applied himself to. Like any normal boy, he loved building forts, romping in the creek near the one home his family lived in for a while, and raking leaves at his grandparents' home.

Charles' grandparents had an incredible influence on him. His paternal grandfather died when he was quite young, so the remaining three grandparents were the ones who helped mold and shape Charles in many ways. He always loved to tell me about the various ways his grandparents loved and nurtured him as a child and young man, helping him learn the value of hard work, diligence, and good time management. Holidays at his grandparents' homes were some of his fondest memories. He would reminisce, telling about the delicious dinners Grandma Wesco would prepare and about the family get-togethers with cousins, aunts, and uncles at his maternal grandparents' home! The love they invested in him during those childhood and young-adult years had a lasting impact on him his entire life.

One of the greatest ways this was evidenced began on Charles' twelfth birthday, when his grandparents gave him his first tuning hammer, and he began learning how to tune pianos at their piano factory. Charles learned quickly how to tune and even at that young age began diligently saving the money he earned to prepare for a home and family of his own someday. By his late teens, he had his own piano tuning and repair business, and this supported him through many years of Bible training and preparation for the ministry. He always told me that he viewed the piano tuning business as a special gift from God, given for a specific purpose—to enable him to be involved in more ministry opportunities. He told me many times it would not always be his to use.

Charles considered Pastor David Miller to be "his pastor." For the majority of his life, he sat under Pastor Miller's ministry at First Baptist Church, Mishawaka, Indiana. After a two-part message Pastor Miller preached, "Those That Are Sent and Those Who Stay," Charles, then fifteen, surrendered to do whatever God called him to do, whether it was ministry in the States or mission work overseas.

Memorizing Scripture truly was one of Charles' greatest passions. He committed most of the New Testament epistles to memory, along with a multitude of other chapters and verses from the Bible. One of the greatest memories I will always hold is remembering how we quoted the book of Philippians together on one of our first dates. Knowing that he was, beyond a shadow of doubt, in an ever-deepening love with the Word of God was always an incredible joy to my heart. About a month before his death, he had decided to begin memorizing the book of Hebrews and was working on the second chapter the day he was martyred.

Charles - the dedicated teenager

Throughout his teenage and early adult years, Charles was actively involved in his church's AWANA program. He loved teaching and loved watching children and young people learn the Word of God. He poured hours not only into the children at church but also into his younger siblings, desiring to see each of them have a heart passion for the Lord. He was intensely involved in helping them with their Scripture memory and also taught them how to do a variety of things, from making bread and different meals to playing choir chimes together. He thrived on anything that could be used as a ministry to others. His mind was constantly focused on discovering new ways to serve God. It was his passion.

In addition to being involved in his local church and receiving his Bible training, Charles devoted a lot of time during his twenties to ministry endeavors. He took several trips to South Africa, and with every trip God increased the love and burden in his heart for the millions of people living in the "Dark Continent."

To Die Is Gain

Playing the accordion

As his thirties approached, Charles sought the Lord's leading in a couple of serious areas—long- term ministry and marriage. He desired to have a wife and family, and he desired to be settled in a ministry. He had experienced many "death of a vision" trials and had finally realized that God was going to have to supernaturally intervene on his behalf. In the summer of 2003, he spent forty days in fasting and prayer, seeking the Lord's face for leading and direction, and casting all his hopes, dreams, and desires before Him.

I had first met Charles and his family when I was twelve and he was twenty-two. Of course, I was too young for him to notice, and I just thought he was a good-looking guy with dark brown eyes and an amazing smile. Other than his family showing up at church for special meetings and his tuning my family's piano, we had had no real interaction with each other. When I was sixteen, though, a close friend of mine, whose husband was preaching evangelistic meetings at our church, told me that she thought Charles and I should get together. I told her there was no way—he was much older and would never notice or be interested in me! Life moved on over the next couple of years as I worked at finishing high school, got involved in the music program of our church, and taught the little children's Sunday school class. Though I still didn't think Charles would ever notice or be interested in me, I always took note of the way he obviously loved the Lord and had a desire to serve Him. I knew that was the kind of man I wanted to marry someday, but that was a long way down the road—or so I thought.

It was late summer or early fall of 2003. The year had held much for me already. I had been deathly ill while trying to complete high school. After getting medical help, my health was on the mend. Graduation was mid-June. Now I was enjoying taking Bible courses and more Spanish as well as teaching piano lessons to a few students. My life was very planned out. I really wanted to complete some Bible courses and then work and save up money to go overseas for a couple of years as a single missionary. By twenty-five or twenty-six, I would be ready to think about marriage.

During our courtship

In November our piano was due for its regular tuning, and our piano tuner, Charles Wesco, came do it as he always did. Normally, after the completion of tuning, he would play a beautiful hymn arrangement, which I always loved. Listening to him play the piano had always left me in awe. (I'll never forget the day years earlier, when I was in high school, and he came to tune the piano. When he was done, he played a beautiful Rudy Atwood arrangement of "When I Survey." As he finished, my sisters and I all leaned back in our school chairs, looked at each other, and said, "Wow!")

But on that November day, Charles asked if there was someone from the family who could play a song for him. At that time, I was the only one in our family who really played the piano, so my father asked me to play something on the freshly tuned instrument. Piano playing had been part of my existence for a long time, so playing something was not that big of a deal. What I did not realize at the time was that my playing the piano that day was what first attracted Charles to me. He told me later that while I was playing, he realized I was someone he thought would make a great wife and partner in ministry, and he began thinking and planning toward that end!

During lunch that day, Charles told us about the Bible study he had been having with a small group from a church in South Bend, Indiana. The church was on the brink of dying, but Charles was so excited about all God was doing and about the possibility of the church being revived, growing, and turning into a thriving body of believers in a very needy community. He threw out the idea to my father that our family should come up to do a special program for some holiday, to help promote the church and get people out to a special service. Valentine's Day was the next possible holiday, and we began preparing for the program a short time later. After lots of practice and singing through many special numbers together, the family was ready. That cold February Sunday afternoon, we drove to South Bend for the Valentine's concert.

Afterwards Charles' family had us over for a meal. Later, as we headed home, my sisters told me that they thought Charles Wesco was definitely interested in me. I told them they were crazy. But the next week and month proved them to be right because he specifically talked about me in his thank-you letter to my dad. He began showing up often at our house and finding ways to get to see us more. I was very confused because he would never single me out, and yet it was obvious that something was there between us. During those weeks, I began seeking the Lord's face earnestly, asking Him for clear direction as to what His will was. I had planned out my life, and this was not in my plan. It left me asking God what He was doing.

Over the next several months, God provided so many desires of my heart as my parents and I saw in Charles a man who loved the Lord with all his heart and desired to serve Him. In early May, it became evident to Charles that I was very interested in him too, but he was headed to South Africa on a mission trip. So, our fathers decided, on my nineteenth birthday, that things would be tabled until his return to the States.

During that month, Charles sent updates of the work he was doing in South Africa. Through those letters, I could see a heart that loved others and desired to see souls reached with the gospel. It gladdened my heart immensely, and I looked forward to Charles' return to the States, when I assumed our relationship would become more official. But in the meantime, I was busily trying to prepare a surprise twentieth wedding anniversary party for my parents in mid-June. One of Charles' sisters loved to decorate and had a variety of things that she graciously agreed to let me use, as well as offering to come and help me decorate.

As weeks went by after his return to the States, and Charles did not contact my dad concerning our relationship, I began to think that perhaps he was no longer interested. I did not know that his parents had told him to wait to do anything more until after my parents' anniversary party was over. He was concerned that almost a month of no contact would convey that he was no longer interested, so he decided to swing by our house once "just to say hi."

I'll never forget him coming through the door and straight over to me, stating as he walked, "Anyone who is willing to be a missionary in Africa someday has to eat one of these!"

In his hand, he held a little plastic bag, containing dried caterpillar-looking worms! Before my brain could think too much about it, I reached in the bag, took one, and ate it. He was not going to win a dare like that with me! I wouldn't find out until after we were married that he himself had never eaten one and had only managed to swallow part of one with a can of Coke. Something about that whole scenario never struck me as fair, and I had very much looked forward to making him a meal of grasshoppers in Cameroon, as payback for getting me to eat a dried worm! That visit will always hold a special place in my heart because somehow that evening, I knew that someday we were going to end up somewhere in Africa as missionaries.

The day for my parents' surprise anniversary party arrived! We had made plans with our assistant pastor and his wife to take my parents out for the day so that we could prepare for the evening. I was horrified that morning when Mom informed me that she wanted us to turn a massive amount of strawberries into freezer jam while she was gone. That had not been part of the plan, but I knew we had to do it. So, we girls went into full production mode and may have set a new record for making a very large amount of strawberry freezer jam in a very short amount of time!

Charles and a couple of his siblings showed up in the afternoon. They pitched in to help my family and so did others from our church, as we finished decorating the auditorium and fellowship hall for the event. Our interaction that day was nearly nonexistent, and I wondered if everything with him was over.

The surprise party was a complete success, and I will always cherish the precious memories we made that evening, celebrating the two people I love and admire more than anyone else in the world. At the end of the evening, I noticed Charles talking to my dad alone. My heart skipped a beat, hoping that perhaps something was going to happen. I found out later that Charles had asked my dad if he could take my parents out to eat to have a chance to talk about our beginning a relationship. They decided to get together the following Monday.

I want to take a moment here to share my heart honestly. Looking back to that Monday is very bittersweet for me. In many ways, it was one of the happiest days of my life since after many hours of talking together, my dad gave his full blessing for Charles and me to begin a courtship relationship. We were so excited to officially begin our relationship. Suddenly, when I looked at Charles, I did not just see a great guy but a great guy who I knew cared deeply about me. My youngest sister, who was four at the time, did not miss a thing and promptly helped get the whole purpose of what was transpiring out in the open when she boldly went over to Charles, climbed up in his lap, and bluntly asked, "Are you going to marry Stephanie?"

There was a round of laughs, and part of me wanted the floor to open up at that moment, but we all smiled as Charles informed her that he was definitely moving in that direction.

3
OUR CHALLENGING COURTSHIP

*A*s I think back, I can see that that day was, in some ways, the beginning of a very special trial God had planned for my life—something I would have run away from if I had known all it would entail in the following months and years. But it was something that God, in His sovereignty, wanted me to go through, to begin to learn on whole new levels, what it means to walk with Jesus and be true to Him and His Word. I had lived a very blessed, sheltered life, in a godly, loving, respectful family, and because of this, I did not comprehend or understand that not all Christian families, who appear to have that same form of godliness, are not, in reality, that way in their hearts and homes. In the early months of our relationship, I began to be faced with this painful reality.

God knew that I needed to experience many invaluable lessons, to walk through tear-filled valleys, and to learn to surrender my expectations and desires in family relationships, though wholly good and right, to Him, and to trust His plan for my life even if it was not all I had hoped for and dreamed of. This realm proved to be the greatest trial in our marriage. The coming months and years would be lacking in much of the joy that should have been there because of unnecessary pain and wounds caused by some people choosing to be controlled by their flesh instead of by the Spirit of God. There would be many dark moments of wondering what God was doing. It would be nearly fifteen years before I would really begin to see God's beautiful purpose and plan in all He was allowing to transpire. He would, in His time, give me a little glimpse into the miraculous and faith-building way He turned those ashes into beauty for His glory and purpose for my life.

During my years of marriage to Charles, when I was asked what we had done on our first date, I had to laugh because it was definitely not your conventional way of getting to know each other. At that time my family raised chickens for meat, and that summer we had around 150 chickens that needed to be butchered a few days after we began dating. So, Charles came to join in on the fun! It was a messy day since there is nothing pretty or glamorous about butchering chickens, but thanks to another dare from the handsome guy I was fast falling for, I cut the head off of one of those poor birds, inwardly promising myself that I would never do it again!

After the project was done and we had cleaned up, my dad took us out to the lake with our family's canoe, and Charles and I went out on the water to enjoy some time talking together. Our faithful chaperone, worn out from a day of hard work, fell asleep on the beach, much to our dismay. Poor Dad got teased about that for a very long time!

That first weekend of our relationship, Charles picked my mom and me up and took us to South Bend for a special outdoor concert followed by fireworks. We stopped at his grandparents' house on the way, and I got to meet them for the first time. They were two of the sweetest people ever, and I immediately felt loved by them. Charles' parents and some of his siblings met us at the concert, and I was so excited to get to spend time with them because I viewed them as some of the godliest people in the whole world and felt so honored at the possibility of being part of their family. The evening went well, and I enjoyed interacting with some of the siblings. Afterwards, we went to Charles' Grandma Wesco's home, where I was to spend the night. Her home was so warm, cozy, and tidy, and I immediately felt welcome. If I remember correctly, she was sick that evening, so I did not get to meet her then. But Charles had told me all about his grandparents, so I felt I already knew her in some ways.

That weekend was difficult for me since it was my first Sunday away from my Sunday school kids, whom I loved very much. There also was some confusion in my heart and mind, due to things that transpired, but every time I looked at the guy who, in just a few days' time, had become extremely important to me, all I could do was smile. My fondest memory from that first weekend and our whole time of courtship was our walk along the dunes on the beach of Lake Michigan. Charles and I both had a serious love of Bible memory, and Philippians was our mutual favorite book to have memorized. So that evening, as we walked, we quoted through the entire book together. I never would have dreamed then that fourteen years later verses from Philippians would be being engraved on his tombstone. I never would have dreamed that the love, happiness, and joy I felt with this man had only a few years to be lived out.

We talked that evening about plans for the future, about what we wanted to see God do in our future family, about the possibility of children, and about wanting to serve the Lord together.

The next couple of months were filled with many ups and downs as my expectations of a beautiful courtship story crumbled. My heart was often in turmoil because relationships I had always dreamed of having ended up becoming messy and uncertain. There would be days of great happiness when I would think everything had leveled out, only to have those hopes dashed and the confusion and uncertainty of our relationship status overwhelm me like a flood. I spent a lot of time seeking the Lord, talking to Charles, and trying to sort through the confusion of not understanding what God was doing and why He was allowing things to go on in the family relationship realm that were wrong. Though I knew I loved Charles with all my heart, I began to wonder if he really did love me. As he sought to honor and obey his parents, the way he had been trained and brought up to do, it would result in my feeling betrayed and unloved. My hopes that he cared for me were dashed. I am so thankful for my dad, who through those days of uncertainly, fear, and confusion, was always there to pray with me and encourage me. Though he and Charles had been good friends long before our relationship started, those days drew them closer together as Dad sought to help, encourage, and challenge Charles in becoming all God wanted him to be as the prospective future husband of his daughter.

We had decided that we would wait to say "I love you" to each other until our engagement, but since his plans to get engaged were cancelled or postponed several times by his parents, I began to wonder if it was just a matter of time until the whole relationship was going to be over. In early August I spent several days with Charles and his family, but due to being placed in several sad and awkward situations, I was left confused and feeling very unstable. I talked with my parents about everything that was happening and poured my heart out to them. Our concerns were the same. They gave me their blessing to share with Charles a special poem I had written for him. The poem ended with, "I love you." I just wanted him to know I loved him, and I wanted to know he loved me too. But he did not say it back to me that evening after I finished reading. He thanked me for the beautiful poem and then tried to simply move on with the evening. I was completely heartbroken that night as I realized that it did not matter how much I loved him; from all appearances, he did not love me that much. What I did not know then was that he spent that whole night in turmoil because he had so wanted to tell me he loved me but was trying to obey and honor his parents. The next day was very strained; I had retreated in my heart from getting hurt again and had begun closing Charles off. I loved him with all my heart, but after feeling like a tug-of-war rope for a couple of months, I was tired of it all. Because of his actions the night before, he knew why I was very reserved and would not open up, and he knew that our relationship would not survive much longer this way.

Without my knowing, my dad had a very long talk with Charles and challenged him to "leave and cleave"—to move forward with the engagement if he wanted me to have any trust in him and his ability to lead a family in the future.

To Die Is Gain

A few days before his thirtieth birthday and after getting permission again from his dad to get engaged, Charles arrived at my family's house with a bouquet of mini roses for me. They were beautiful, and he told me later that he got mini ones because they had more petals, which could be redeemed for kisses on our wedding day! We drove up to Syracuse, Indiana, to the beautiful Oakwood Resort, where Charles had rented a big pontoon boat for everyone to go out on the lake together. Unfortunately, due to all the tension that was in his family over our engagement, they refused to come and be part of the event. Charles had purchased a cooler full of delicious food and snacks, which made my sisters and brothers very happy. Food is always a heart winner with future younger siblings-in-law.

The day was beautiful, sunny, and warm, and there was excitement in my heart when Charles asked me to take a walk with him along the edge of the lake. Part of me was totally prepared for another disappointment, but part of me really hoped today was actually going to be "the day!"

We came to a bench, where there was a wrapped box, and we both sat down together. He handed me a beautiful little inlaid wooden ring box. I do not remember everything he said, but I do remember him reading me a beautiful card, saying, "I love you," and then asking me the question I had dreamed of hearing from him: "Stephanie, will you marry me?"

Our engagement ring

Inside the card, beautiful handwritten text said:

My darling Stephanie!

This card reflects my heart about you so perfectly! Stephanie, you are a gift directly from the Lord to me. You have encouraged me over the past year so very much. Thank you for always believing in me like you have. Thank you for your sweet and meek spirit, smiling countenance, and trusting demeanor. I know you are eager to grow more, but I already see you as a woman of virtue and prudence. I have been so spurred on in my determination and love for the Lord and His work through the influence that you have had upon my life already!

I am thrilled beyond measure and so excited about our November 20 wedding! I know that, Lord willing, I will get many more opportunities to grow in expressing my love for you, Stephanie, throughout all our lives. But I just want to say again that I love you, my dearest, more than anything else or anyone else, other than God. Please continue to be patient with me as I learn more and more over the next few months what it means to begin cleaving to you. I am now committed to spending the rest of my life together with you, and I make this commitment to you with great joy and viewing it as a great privilege and favor from my Savior!

I gave a hearty yes to Charles' question, and he motioned for me to open the box. There inside was the engagement ring he had picked for me. It was a more beautiful ring than I had ever dreamed of wearing, and as it slid onto my finger, I realized this was really happening! There was so much joy in my heart at that moment as we prayed together, asking the Lord to remain the focus of our lives together and surrendering our future to Him. Charles also gave me a beautiful new Bible that matched his, with my name engraved on the front. Today I use that Bible for our family devotions, and I try to remember, as I seek to continue raising our children, how we vowed to God that day to have a family that would serve God wholeheartedly.

Later that evening we all drove to a horse show, where a few of Charles' siblings met up with us. I could tell there was tension in the air with them but could not figure out what was wrong since Charles had tried to keep the day as carefree and beautiful for me as possible. Within a few days, the truth of the severity of the situation would surface, and the beauty and joy of our engagement day would be hidden from view with more storm clouds.

The next week was exciting but difficult as I began working hard to prepare for our wedding day. We started making lists of all that needed to be done in the next three months. In the middle of all that, the tension in Charles' family over our relationship and engagement reached a boiling point. It left me bewildered, broken, and utterly confused when I realized how serious things were. On Charles' birthday, in order to try to appease Charles' parents, my parents went out to eat with them. That meeting revealed many issues of the heart. When I look back at things that were said to my parents at that time, I have to surrender everything to God again. I have to remember that God allowed it, but I know, beyond a shadow of doubt, it grieved His heart. The Lord had an ultimate and perfect plan He was working out, both in Charles' life and mine, because He was working to shape and mold us into the vessels, He wanted us to be. I'll never forget the special joy that filled my heart that day, though, as Charles' siblings came down, and we all had a birthday celebration for him. I adored him, and the fact that he had chosen me was almost unbelievable.

The following months brought many ups and downs. My mom was busy trying to make the bridesmaids' dresses while being pregnant with my little brother and homeschooling my younger siblings! I will forever be so grateful for all that my parents sacrificed for me throughout those months. We had decided to get married at the church where Charles had grown up and had always dreamed of getting married—First Baptist Church in Mishawaka. Pastor Miller and his wife were two of the sweetest, godliest people I knew, and the Lord used them to strengthen and stabilize me over those few months. Pastor Miller was our marriage counselor, and Mrs. Miller graciously agreed to be our wedding coordinator. They both played an even larger role than I think they ever realized in helping Charles and me prepare for our marriage and wedding day.

Amid all the wedding planning craziness, we also began looking for a house. Charles had diligently saved for a home and family from the time he was twelve and wanted to purchase a house debt-free. One evening, I received a call from him regarding the possibility of purchasing a fixer-upper that his brother had found. The state was going to demolish it, so it would have to be moved to another piece of land and then have a lot of work done on the inside. After a visit to Mishawaka and a good sales pitch from Charles' brother, I agreed to the idea, and thus we began a huge undertaking that would not be completely finished for a couple of years. The house-moving was incredible to observe as it was literally hauled down the road, across a field, and set down on a piece of land less than a mile away. It took many hours of hard work and many helping hands from family, friends, and acquaintances for it to be even livable when we returned from our honeymoon in mid-December.

Charles had spent hours, days, months, and years building and remodeling his parents' house as a young man, so he loved this undertaking, pouring hours into redoing a bathroom that was falling apart, retiling half of the main floor, and doing his best to turn the house into a home for me. I have to smile, remembering the day I stood in the master bathroom, fighting with wallpaper that seemed to have been super-glued to the wall. Hearing a saw out in the hallway, I walked out to see Charles cutting out the main bathroom wall. Completely freaked out, I asked him what in the world he was doing? He calmly replied that there was no other way to get the new tub/shower unit into the bathroom, and that he would simply put the wall back in place when they were done installing the new unit. I did not find that very comforting, seeing as our wedding was only a few weeks away, and he was cutting out a very necessary wall. But he did it, and before I knew it, the wall was back in place, mudded, and ready to be painted.

Watching Charles work on the house made me fall in love with him even more as I saw how much he cared about preparing a home for me. He poured his heart into it. Even though we spent that first winter without a real septic system, looking at large mounds of snow-covered dirt instead of a yard, a complete drop-off outside the patio door, a path of mud instead of a sidewalk, and no functioning laundry room, we were so happy in our own house. We were working on it little by little, making it our own. Because of that project, when the children and I would return from Cameroon, almost exactly fourteen years later, living in a house that needed work did not freak me out. I am so thankful for all God taught me throughout that process.

In the midst of preparations for our wedding day, Charles shared with me that he had a desire to go to Cameroon after we were married. It would be a long-term mission trip of nine months or so. I was excited at the prospect even though it was full of unknowns, and we began getting the necessary shots and paperwork together. Our plans came to a standstill, though, when we were informed that one of the immunizations could lead to serious birth defects if I were to get pregnant even many months after having the shot. We both wanted to have a family right away, so after praying about it, we believed God was closing the door for the trip at that time and chose to follow the direction He seemed to be leading, with Charles serving as an assistant pastor to his father.

Bridal showers, wedding details, and house preparations during the last few weeks before the wedding were mixed with continued tension and high stress, and I could tell from the pain hitting my body that it was taking its toll. The week before the wedding was a roller coaster of emotions. Leaving my parents and siblings to marry the man I loved was bittersweet, especially due to the stress level. That was not Charles' fault, but it was there, nonetheless.

One evening, just a few days before the wedding, I reached a breaking point when demands were placed on me regarding wedding details, and Charles told me to concede. I poured my heart out to my dad, and though he was in agreement with me on the situation, he was wise in his response. He did not counsel me against the wishes of the man I was about to marry but instead strongly encouraged me to share my heart with Charles the way I had with him. It was very hard to do because it involved his family members, but I am so thankful my dad encouraged me to confide in Charles before our wedding day. His response was calm, loving, understanding, and comforting even though we did not agree about how the situation should be handled. I chose to obey him, and he told me that my respect and obedience to his wishes, even when I did not agree with him, had meant more to him than I could even imagine. Though I had known it before, I realized again that day, that God had given me a man who was not angry or hasty. He was patient and filled with "the wisdom that is from above." He had baggage from being raised with a mindset that required an unbiblical level of "honor," "obedience," and "submission," but he loved me and truly wanted me to be happy.

Our wedding day dawned cold and rainy—not exactly what I had dreamed of, but by that time, I did not care a bit how dreary the weather was. I was marrying the man I loved with my whole heart, and the rain did not hamper my joy at all. We arrived at the church and everyone began the preparation process. Excitement ran high as my aunt and mom helped me get ready. Charles and I had agreed to not see each other before the ceremony, which added to the anticipation.

Finally, the moment arrived. As the doors opened, my dad and I walked hand in hand down the aisle toward the man I would soon call "husband." Even though he was smiling with a light in his eyes, I could see that he was crying. Throughout the entire ceremony, there was no greater joy for me than to look into the eyes of the one my soul loved as I vowed to him—before God—to love, honor, and obey, for richer or poorer, in sickness, and in health, till death did us part. Our first kiss was a bit rough since Charles completely pulled my veil off, necessitating a quick fix and resulting in lots of laughter from the audience. There would definitely be no issues in the kissing department!

We were pronounced "Mr. and Mrs. Charles Wesco," and as we walked out of the auditorium husband and wife, I really believed that I could never be happier than I was at that moment.

As we exited the church to begin our honeymoon, Charles read to me from the Song of Solomon, "Arise my love, my beautiful love, and come away with me!"

To Die Is Gain

Mr. & Mrs. Wesco

The honeymoon was a very special time away together in almost every respect. Unfortunately, all of the built-up stress took its toll, and I spent the first week very sick and unable to eat anything. But the Lord was good in that after lots of fluids, vitamin C, rest, and sleep, I began feeling normal again. Most of our time together was spent on the southern coastline of California and northern Mexico, and I loved our walks along the beach of the Pacific Ocean, where it was so beautiful and calm. The only part of our honeymoon that we never came to an agreement on was that of a day of fasting Charles thought we should do. I did not think a honeymoon was the greatest time for such a day, but he told me I needed to trust him and obey, so I did. Years later, we would have fun playfully arguing about it since neither one of us ever changed our opinion on the subject.

We returned to our new home late one night in mid-December. As we entered the house, I was stunned at its transformation. It looked clean and tidy—very different from the last time I had been there the week of the wedding. I discovered later that my sweet new sister-in-law, who had married Charles' younger brother earlier that year, had recruited some of the younger brothers-in-law, and they had cleaned up the house for us the best they could. It meant so much to walk into a tidy house and helped immensely with the homesickness I was already feeling.

4
OUR HEAVEN ON EARTH

Those early days of marriage were truly "heaven on earth!" Setting up and furnishing our new home consumed much of our time. We were immensely happy. Around New Year's Day, I started feeling extremely nauseous and just wanted to sleep constantly, and we discovered a week later that we were about to enter the next phase of life—being a daddy and mommy. Both of us had wanted to have a large family and were very excited about it and thankful to the Lord for this first precious baby God was giving us. We both hoped for a firstborn son and knew immediately he would be a "Daniel." That was the name we both had wanted for our first son before we were even a couple.

That first pregnancy was very hard, as most first pregnancies are. I struggled with extreme nausea, exhaustion, and severe swelling. It is almost humorous now to think about church services when I would run to the bathroom to vomit after the first song and during the opening prayer and then get back to the piano in time to play the next hymn. That was my life as a nauseous first-time mom/church pianist.

Charles loved having a partner in ministry, and we thoroughly enjoyed having people from the church over to our home for meals, starting soon after our wedding. We were very involved in the music ministry, and I loved playing the piano for the church services. We did piano duets together and had so much fun preparing and then playing them at church. Charles loved to study and preach, and I loved watching him spend time with his heavenly Father. Serving the Lord together made us so happy and fulfilled!

I was so thankful that even though there were still periods of tension, the relationship with his family stabilized for the most part after our wedding, and we were our own independent family and home. I loved having his family over for meals and tried to find ways to let them know that I truly loved and cared for them. The Lord gave a me great joy and peace in doing that, and I knew it made Him happy.

That first summer of marriage, we planted a big garden and had more watermelon and butternut squash than we could handle. What a wonderful problem to have! Many evenings were spent pulling weeds, picking produce, and having fun outside together.

In early September of 2004, after reading about and preparing for the birth of our first baby, my body began playing with labor. It turned into a multiple-day process, and we were so thankful to God for His protection and deliverance when after a very long, hard labor, our firstborn son, Daniel Donald, entered this world, weighing just a little over seven pounds. He was named for his daddy and mommy's Bible hero as well as for my father.

Charles, Daniel and I - shortly after Daniel was born

I do not remember a lot from the first days when he was brand-new because my body was completely worn out from the delivery, and it took days for me to even feel human again. He was a sweet, petite baby, who had his daddy's brown eyes and loved to take naps with Mommy, but he took life very seriously right from the beginning. He was very alert but liked having peace and quiet. His personality started reminding me of his daddy very quickly since he was never content at the baby stage as normal babies would be. As soon as he rolled, he wanted to scoot, and so on, with each stage of development. His love for music also showed up at a very young age. At nine months, he would wake up early in the morning and start singing the tunes to Scripture songs I had taught him. Charles would shake his head in amazement, and I would smile, realizing God had answered my prayers for my baby to love music and singing. Charles jokingly told me, since it was very evident that Daniel was going to be a leader to any future siblings, that we should just name our next three sons Hananiah, Mishael, and Azariah, like Daniel's three friends in the Bible. I told him that no one had four boys in a row and that those were not my first picks for my sons' names, but the thought of having four boys in a row made me laugh because it sounded so unreal. Little did I realize, that within four years, God would get the last laugh and bless me with my four oldest children—all boys!

When Daniel was six months old, we found out he was going to be a big brother since God had blessed us with another child, who was due around Thanksgiving of 2006. We were very excited, and Charles informed me, that if this baby was a boy, he would be a Junior. I was hoping for a girl the second time around but mainly asked the Lord for a healthy baby.

In God's goodness, the second labor and delivery went smoothly and fairly quickly. Our second child, Charles Truman Jr., weighed in at over a pound more than his big brother and had beautiful blue eyes and a head of brown hair, with blond around the edges of his forehead. He was my little cuddle bug right from the beginning and loved being mommy's constant buddy. It was very evident that his personality was the complete opposite of his big brother, who was already trying to be a man at fourteen months old. His cry melted my heart, and his brother was always very concerned every time he heard a whimper. I loved my two little boys and felt like my world was perfect in so many ways. Daniel and Charles Jr. complimented each other's strengths and weaknesses, even as a toddler and baby, and they became best playmates right away.

Charles with his namesake - Charles Jr.

While Charles Jr. was a baby, Charles decided it was time to finish our basement. He spent hours working on it with help from a young man who was attending our church at the time. Before long, we had a beautiful finished basement. I enjoyed using it to host our church's first bridal shower, for a girl who was marrying a young man in the church. During those months the Lord gave me a strong sense that He had a specific purpose in mind for that basement, and I began praying that God would show Charles His plan and purpose for it. In the meantime, we loved having more space for when our families would come over for meals and birthday parties. It definitely made hospitality a lot easier for us.

Our family of four

Summer of 2007 found me feeling nauseous again, and after two pregnancies, I was fairly certain God had blessed us again. Those suspicions turned out to be accurate when a pregnancy test confirmed that baby number three was coming in April of 2008! This time, Charles left the baby naming up to me, and I asked him if we could do an ultrasound this time and find out the baby's gender, to which he agreed. I honestly was hoping for another boy and was very excited when the technician confirmed that our active baby was indeed a boy.

The Lord blessed me with a wonderful pregnancy, but it became a bit embarrassing during the last several months because I was often asked when I was due and if it was twins. I knew I was big, but not that big! The due date came and went, and still there was no baby. After going three days early with my first two, I just thought the third would kindly follow in his big brothers' footsteps, but no! He wanted to forge his own path, and two weeks late, Joseph Nathaniel arrived, after making Mommy work hard to get him out. As my midwife laid him on me, all I could say was, "He's so big!" The nurse agreed and guessed he was going to weigh in at nine pounds. My midwife decided to not even guess. Joseph wanted to curl up with Mommy and nurse immediately, but when an hour had come and gone, and he was still nursing strong, the nurse came and took him to clean him up, which made him very upset. Eating was evidently very important to him—it still is! I'll never forget my midwife coming in and saying,

"Stephanie, I am so sorry." When I questioned why she would say such a thing, she informed me that my little boy had weighed in at nine pounds and fourteen ounces, and if he had waited for his first diaper filling till after they had weighed him, she was sure he would have been well over ten pounds. Now we knew why his delivery had been a lot more work. She said, "I never would have dreamed you could birth that big a baby, but you did!"

Charles and Joseph

I knew then how good God had been to give me another son and a beautiful birth with no complications. Joseph quickly proved to be the easiest, happiest, and best baby I ever had. He started grinning from ear to ear at barely three weeks, but his daddy was convinced it was gas. I was sure that it was not, but that God had just given us the happiest baby ever. Both facts were probably true, but Joseph soon became our cheerful, bubbly baby. He loved being happy, and even at that age, he loved seeing other people happy. He has never lost his fun-loving personality, and to this day, he keeps us well entertained with his sense of humor, contagious laugh, and big smile.

Joseph had always been one of my favorite Bible characters since he exemplified a life of faith, service, and surrender—with nothing negative recorded about him. Nathaniel, who was one of Jesus' disciples, was labeled by Jesus as one in whom there was no guile. That was my prayer for this son from before his birth, and I continue to pray that he will seek to follow in the footsteps of the men he was named after.

That summer was so much fun with three little boys age two and under. There was not a dull moment around our house ever! Charles loved having his little men and spent a lot of time reading to them and playing with them. Being their daddy was one of his greatest dreams come true, and I loved watching him be their daddy. I was very happy and content with my three-little people, and with being a boy mom, but I really hoped our next baby would be a little girl.

During those days of learning what life looked like with three little ones, God gave me the beautiful gift of ladies in the church, who set before me incredible examples of being godly, faithful mothers. Their encouragement and advice were such a tremendous help to me in those early days as a mom, and one of those ladies became a very good friend, who to this day holds the "best friend" status. Rhonda Hicks and I had first met when she was expecting her ninth child and I was expecting Daniel. Her sweet spirit and demeanor always encouraged me and watching her mother her children truly showed me the example of a Proverbs 31 woman.

Charles and Steve Hicks were kindred spirits too, always enjoying spending time together. In 2014, the year before we would start deputation for Cameroon, Charles began teaching Steve how to tune and do everything he knew about working with pianos. In 2018, the piano tuning and repair business would become officially Steve's to carry on. From the earliest days of our friendship, the Hicks family was always fun to spend time with, and their daughters became such blessings to me, as they began helping me around the house, and earned the "best babysitters in the world" award. They mirrored all their parents had invested in them, and to this day, my kids' best friends are a "bunch of Hicks"!

God answered one of my prayers that summer. He laid on Charles' heart the need to start a Bible institute at our church to train the young people in God's Word and hopefully give them tools they could carry throughout life to serve the Lord. Such great joy filled my heart when Charles asked me what I would think about using our basement as the place for the classes to meet. I was so excited and shared with him how the Lord had laid a burden on my heart for the basement to be used for Him and how I had been praying. So that fall, Tuesday evenings found our basement filled with young men and some of their fathers taking theology courses together. My job was to make snack foods for the students and keep my little one's quiet upstairs. Those months will always be treasured memories for me as God gave us the privilege of seeing Him use our home to be a place where people gathered to learn about Him.

Charles teaching in the Bible Institute

Charles also spent hours preparing a Bible memory program based on the verses he had learned through AWANA as a child, and it became an incredible tool for helping our children as well as other kids in the church to hide multiple Scripture verses and passages in their hearts.

But all was not honey and roses throughout 2008 because the fairly stable relationship with Charles' family began to spiral downward in the summer and fall of that year. There were clear reasons for it, which completely broke my heart as I realized how much had been masked and covered over, for the most part, during the first four years of our marriage. Though Charles knew things were not right, there were many aspects of relationships, where abnormal had been his normal for so many years, and he could not clearly see what was happening. Though our marriage was still strong, and we were still very much in love, some things in our relationship became strained as an evil spirit of contention, criticism, and discord spread in his family, away from the public eye. I hated hypocrisy and could not understand why it was just considered normal, OK, and almost righteous. I hated that my husband's spirit towards me would change from one of unconditional love and acceptance to one of judgment, criticism, and comparing after he had spent time with certain members of his family. I did not understand why he seemed OK with behavior that was clearly sin just because of who was doing it. No matter how much I tried to point out to him where it seemed things were so messed up, he did not see it and reached the point of being very irritated and upset with me for not just going along with things.

As the situation worsened over the coming year, I came to realize that God would have to intervene because I could not open my husband's eyes. After many tears and crying out to the Lord for help in the middle of so much pain and confusion, I began to ask God to open Charles' eyes to how things really were. I also asked the Lord to open my eyes because part of me truly wondered if Charles was right and I was completely off my rocker in what I was seeing. Nothing truly changed for the better in the situation, and because I had been told numerous times to "be the rug," that slowly became my norm. I found an odd sense of happiness in just closing my eyes, ears, and mouth and trying to simply go along most of the time with the flow of madness.

At the end of February in 2009, I was very surprised to get a positive result on a pregnancy test. We had not prayed for another baby yet, but we were very excited at the prospect of another precious little one. My children had become my complete world in many respects and thinking about having another baby around made me so happy. I had not felt sick at all yet, though, and we were headed to a Bible conference in Wisconsin. I picked up a cold virus that week, which left me sick in bed with a fever part of the time. When we got home, I started having signs of a miscarriage. My heart broke, thinking that God was taking my baby. As the symptoms worsened, we began crying out to God for a miracle. The Lord brought us both to the point of being convinced that He had a special purpose for this baby's life, and we began specifically asking the Lord that, if He would give us this baby, the child would grow up to be an evangelist who would lead many people to know Him as their Savior. I should have known that meant I was asking for another boy. God has a sense of humor.

When my symptoms got worse, I called my midwife to ask her if I could go into the hospital to speed up the miscarriage process because we were supposed to be going to Florida the following week. She was okay with that as long as we did an ultrasound first to ensure the baby was indeed dead. I almost laughed, telling her I did not know how a baby could survive this, but she assured me there was a possibility of it. She scheduled the ultrasound, and we found ourselves holding our breath as the technician looked for the heartbeat. I could not believe my ears, as she happily said, "There it is! That tiny movement is the heart beating!"

It truly was a miracle that she had found the heartbeat, given how early I was. I truly believe it was God who showed it to us to preserve the life of our fourth child. I went into heavy labor for hours that afternoon and just lay weeping, asking the Lord why He would allow us to see our baby's heartbeat, just to take him away, while at the same time, begging Him to let me keep this precious little one. I had to give my precious baby back to God that day and trust that He would do what was best.

A week passed, the bleeding stopped, and my morning sickness kicked in at high gear. Never before had I been so happy to be sick and bent over the toilet vomiting. A few months later, we got to see our baby again on the ultrasound and found out that it was indeed another boy! At first, I cried, a bit disappointed, but the Lord smacked me upside the head, reminding me of the incredible miracle this little boy was and of the prayer I had made to Him, regarding the life purpose of my son. Immediately, I asked God to forgive me for being so ungrateful and promised to do my best to raise this precious little boy to be a man of God. Though he was due the end of October, Hudson Taylor Wesco, named after one of his daddy's missionary heroes, did not make his appearance until very early one November morning, weighing in around nine and a half pounds.

Charles and Hudson Taylor

Life was a bit crazy with four little men, ranging from a four-year-old to a newborn, but it was a fun life, and I loved being a mommy. Daniel and Charles Jr. were in preschool and loved it. Our kitchen table was craft central station as we learned Bible verses, the alphabet, made puppets, colored, and had so much fun together. Joseph did very well at keeping himself occupied with his toys, and as soon as he could hold a pencil, we noticed he was always trying to draw something. Then there was Hudson, the youngest member of "the Fabulous Four." He was a good baby, very content to be in the sling with Mommy or to lie in his bed. He kept Mommy busy doing laundry because he got the first-place award among our babies for projectile vomiting after eating.

God had begun answering one of the biggest prayers of my heart that summer of 2009. True to His Word, He is not willing that any should perish, but that all should come to repentance. He drew my two oldest sons to Himself. One morning, Daniel and Charles Jr. came to me in the kitchen, informing me that they wanted to get saved. We went into the living room, sat down, and began talking through the plan of salvation together. They already knew all the verses since those were some of the first ones, I had taught them. After unsuccessfully trying to distract them, testing to see if this was for real, I realized they were very serious about wanting to make this decision. I listened and cried, and my two oldest children, one after the other, gave their hearts to Jesus and asked Him to forgive their sin and wash their hearts clean. Watching God so clearly work in their hearts astounded me. There was an immediate change in their behavior that day. In little areas where I felt I was hitting a wall in child-training, suddenly they were very concerned about obeying and pleasing Jesus. The wonder of the new heart and desires God gives at salvation, even in a child, never gets old.

Trials come in different forms, and for some reason the Lord has allowed one form to be my lot more times than I would have chosen —broken bones.

One cold morning in early 2010, as I walked up our sloping driveway, I slipped on the ice and caught myself with my left hand. I knew immediately something was wrong and called Charles, who was out tuning pianos. He had to finish his tuning, so I called my family. My sister asked me if I felt like I was going to vomit, which I confirmed. She told me she thought I probably had broken something, which was not what I wanted to hear, but it was confirmed by an x-ray later that day. Since I had four little boys, he put me in a cast to protect the small wrist fracture while it healed. Hudson was still a newborn, and it broke my heart that I could no longer nurse him, and it was very hard to find a comfortable way to hold him. My family offered to watch the three older boys for a short time while I tried to figure out life with the cast. God was good, and it healed in the time the doctor was hoping, and after more time in a brace, my wrist felt almost as good as new.

That spring we were visiting my family for a day, and I was telling my sisters how I was fighting being really tired. They informed me that they were sure I was pregnant again. I was completely shocked and informed them that there was no way. Hudson was not even six months old yet, and that would make five kids five and under. They gave me the all-knowing sister look, and the conversation changed direction.

That evening, as we were traveling home, I started feeling extremely carsick, and I got a knot in my stomach—something that only happened when I was pregnant. We got home and while Charles was busy in his office, I quickly went and took a pregnancy test, just to comfort myself with a negative. Instead, when I looked at the test a few minutes later, it was positive! I could not believe it, and I knew Charles was going to be shocked. Sure enough, when I told him I thought we were expecting another baby, he responded, "That test must have been defective. There's no way!"

After trying multiple brands, all of which came back positive, he realized we were indeed having a surprise baby. But we had absolutely no idea when I was due, so we had an ultrasound done, to be able to confirm the timeframe our midwife thought was accurate, and the ultrasound gave a Christmas Day due date. The ultrasound also resulted in the biggest shock of our lives.

"It's a little girl!" Those were words I never expected to hear after four boys in a row, and I was in shock for the remainder of the procedure. There was lots of excitement as we got to go shopping for pinks, purples, dresses, cute bows, and all things girly. Charles was a little nervous about having a girl and informed me immediately, that he wanted his little girl named after her mommy. I tried to protest, but in the end, we compromised. Stephanie Joyanna had the name Daddy wanted and her middle name was the name Mommy wanted!

She arrived Christmas morning, bringing tears of joy to our faces, as we took in the beauty of our first daughter. She was born blue, due to the cord being around her neck. She had to have oxygen, but—praise the Lord—she was OK and began returning to a normal healthy color within a short amount of time. I was a little shocked when I lifted her up to see that my little girl had a full head of thick, long, dark black hair and dark skin. She looked absolutely nothing like me. The nurse told me, "If I hadn't just seen you birth that baby, I would swear she wasn't yours!"

Our great Christmas present - with baby Stephanie (called Stephy)

After my big boys, she was such a petite little thing, weighing a few ounces shy of eight pounds. We fell in love with her immediately, but I had to get used to hearing her daddy call her "Sweetie," which up to that point had been his name for me.

Stephy Joy, as her name quickly became, was a serious baby, mimicking her oldest brother in many ways. But we also discovered that she had a severe allergy to any type of dairy product as well as to chocolate. As long as I avoided every single form of those things, she was a much happier baby. Her intensity left me bewildered sometimes because I had envisioned a little girl who was always happy and easy going. But as she got older, she leveled out, and now she is such a sweetheart with a kind, caring, loving, and giving spirit.

While I was pregnant with Stephy, I knew we had to make some adjustments if life was to run smoothly at all with five little children. Daniel was an extremely responsible five-year-old, and a couple of months before Stephy's birth, I instituted "the buddy system" in our home. Hudson, who was not even one yet, became Daniel's buddy. I taught him how to help Hudson get his coat and shoes on, along with constantly reminding him that it was his responsibility to help get Hudson drinks, snacks, or toys, as well as looking out for him. Hudson was not even walking yet and was a danger to himself. Daniel took that job very seriously and did a superb job being the big brother buddy to Hudson. Even though there were still many things I had to do for Hudson, just having that little bit of help from Daniel went such a long way. When Stephy was born, Charles Jr. became her buddy, and I was shocked at how seriously he took the job, as barely a four-year-old. He was loving and caring with her and was constantly looking out for her every need. Two-and-a-half-year-old Jolly Joseph stayed my buddy, but he felt very left out, not having a little buddy of his own. I assured him that when God gave us our next baby, that would be his buddy, to which he replied, "When is God going to give me my buddy?"

Oh my! I told him it would be a while—I hoped.

But June of 2011 found me sick again. After a positive pregnancy test, I was feeling very overwhelmed with life, and for the first time, I did not thank God for the precious gift of another child. Within a few days, I knew something was seriously wrong, and when I took another test, it was negative. My heart broke, realizing that my baby was gone, and I had never even treasured that baby's life. I named the baby Hosanna, as I thought of him or her being with Jesus, singing praises to Him. It was over a month before my body decided to even try to let go of the baby, and for the next several months, there was obviously something wrong. In early December, I finally miscarried what was left of the pregnancy. It broke my heart to realize I had been farther along than I had previously thought, and in some ways, it felt like another miscarriage. How sweet the hope of heaven became to me during those days, realizing that my sweet baby was safe with Jesus.

God gives the richest spiritual blessings in the midst of the deepest emotional and physical pain. One evening that fall, during family devotions, we had just finished singing "One Door and Only One" together, when Joseph looked at his daddy and said with a very serious face, "Daddy, I am on the outside!"

Joseph thinks mostly in pictures. He had started memorizing verses as a two-year-old and thus had most of the salvation verses memorized. He had seen himself on the wrong side of "the Door." Before ten minutes had passed, it was very evident that Joseph understood his need to accept Jesus as his Savior, and Charles got the privilege of leading our third born son to Jesus. Several years later, Joseph became very scared because he could not clearly remember that day when he was three. He asked Jesus to save him again, giving him peace and assurance of salvation. "But Jesus said, Suffer little children, and forbid them not, to come unto me: for of such is the kingdom of heaven" (Matthew 19:14). Nothing is more precious than hearing your children come to Jesus for salvation from sin, with that simple, trusting dependence.

I began asking the Lord for another child, another chance to be a mommy. I promised to love and train that child up for Him. God heard and answered those prayers, and we found out in January of 2012 that we were going to have another baby, due to arrive in September. I was sicker than I had been with any of the previous pregnancies, which resulted in my losing over fifteen pounds in the first two trimesters. We decided to let this baby be a surprise, but I really was hoping for a boy again. Charles had found a cell phone app that he was very excited to try out during my labor. It was supposed to tell you where you were in the process of labor progression. I laughed and told him no phone app would be able to read my body, but I had to eat those words.

Samuel's labor started out nice and easy, and I functioned fairly normally throughout the day, thinking it would be twenty-four hours or so before things got serious. By the evening, Charles could tell from his phone app that things were progressing faster than I thought. I told him he was crazy, but I am very thankful that he listened to his app. Otherwise Samuel Paul-David would have made his appearance in the car! Charles' sister came over to stay with the children in the middle of the night, and we arrived at the birthing center with thirty minutes to spare, early that mid-September morning. God blessed us with a beautiful, safe birth, and I think there were extra tears shed as I heard his little cry and thanked God for the precious gift of my seventh child and sixth one here on earth! Samuel was a perfect weight, a little less than nine pounds, and proved to be a very healthy, easy, cheerful, content baby—my constant reminder of God's goodness. He truly was "asked of God" like Samuel in the Bible and was also named after the assistant pastor of my church, who had been like a second dad to me.

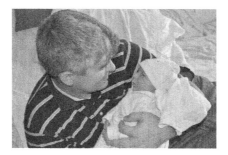

Charles & Samuel

As we entered the Fall of that year, neither Charles nor I dreamed how deep the valley was into which God was taking us. We never would have thought that in a few short months we would no longer be in the ministry we loved so dearly.

5

BROKEN

Shortly before Samuel's birth, Charles' father, who was dealing with Parkinson's, unexpectedly announced that his days as pastor of the church were numbered and that he would be asking the church to consider one of his sons, who were serving as assistant pastors, to become the new pastor of the church. Charles came home that day and cried. He loved serving under his dad and would have been content to do so many more years. Over the next several weeks, my heart broke as God began to reveal to Charles the realities and severity of the situation that he had been blind to for so long. God was beginning to answer my prayers for my husband's eyes to be opened, but watching my husband's heart be broken was so hard.

For months we kept serving as we watched warning signs increase and God's direction increasingly point away from the ministry, we were in. God allowed some events to transpire that served to confirm in our hearts and minds that we were not on the same path with the rest of the family and church leadership. We began fasting and praying, seeking God's clear direction. Charles realized that the Lord was taking him down a path that had never been in his life's plan but one that was necessary to be a true disciple of his Savior.

In the middle of the upheaval, I began having signs of another impending miscarriage. I knew that the stress of everything going on was not helping anything, but I could not relieve the stress and tearfully surrendered to whatever God's will was for my baby. In early May, on the wedding day of one of Charles' siblings, I finally went into labor and miscarried there at the church. Someday I look forward to meeting my precious Peace, named for the comfort God filled my heart with that day when I had to put on a fake face even though my heart was breaking inside.

The next several days were filled with pain for us as a couple because the following day Charles preached his last sermon to the people he loved so much. It was based on Philippians 1:21: "For to me to live is Christ, and to die is gain."

He knew his life had to be about loving, honoring, obeying, and serving Christ above anyone or anything else. The Lord had brought him to the next level of discipleship. God had removed the scales from his eyes, and my heart broke, knowing the pain he felt as he pled with the people he loved to live for Christ, to follow where He led, and to let nothing in this world hold their hearts and devotion. As I listened to him preach that Sunday with my own heart breaking, I had to thank the Lord for answering my prayers by leading my husband and making him into an even greater man of God. He had often challenged the young people at the church to be willing to go wherever God called them, even out of their comfort zone and into the unknown; now he was getting ready to lead by example, and I knew God was going to bless him for it.

That week he resigned from his position as assistant pastor. I will never forget the pain that filled both of our hearts. We loved the people and the ministry there, but we knew we could not continue to go along with mindsets and actions that were unbiblical. Separation is not fun, easy, or pleasant, but Christians must always obey God rather than men, no matter the cost. The next couple of months we learned firsthand what it meant to "be made of no reputation" as we were slandered and falsely accused by some of the people we loved most. God broke us during those days, drawing us much closer to Himself and each other.

We joined and began attending my father's church, where I had been raised, in Warsaw, Indiana. We were hurting deeply, and it took several months before the repercussions of our decision to follow God's leading began to calm down.

Sometime during those weeks of fiery trial, the Lord gave me a poem one evening while I was washing dishes and talking to Him.

In Christ We Will Trust

Trust in God with all your heart
And lean not on your own understanding.
In all your ways acknowledge Him,
And He will direct your paths.
For My ways are not your ways,
And My thoughts are not your thoughts.
We are clay in our Potter's hand—
His Master design He has planned.
For me to live is my Lord
And with His heart be in one accord.
This day we have chosen to serve our God!
He our family deserves!

Refrain:
O Lord, we trust in You! We know You will see us through!
Though we can't see Your Master plan, we'll trust in Your
*   almighty hand.*
O Lord, You're our strength and song. You know the right
*   from wrong.*
And when our way looks bleak, Your Word we will trust
*   and seek—For Lord, You are our God! In You we will*
*   trust!*

—Stephanie Wesco

Charles, who never let grass grow under his feet, loved getting involved in helping in our new church. He helped get a Bible memory program running and began going out on the Sunday afternoon outreaches. His hope was that eventually the Lord would lead him to a new church as a pastor, but in the meantime, he stayed busy serving the Lord any way he could. Opportunities for possible pastoral positions came up in the next few months, but the Lord clearly closed those doors. In spite of setbacks from a human perspective, Charles stayed focused on serving the Lord where He had planted us, investing hours of prayer, love, and energy into his children, the young people of the church, a young man he had led to the Lord and was seeking to disciple as well as anyone else God put in his path.

That summer brought the blessing of another one of our precious children becoming part of God's family. As at the end of family devotions one evening, Hudson came over to me and told me that he needed to ask Jesus to come into his heart. He clearly understood he was a sinner and needed God's forgiveness. That evening I had the privilege of leading another one of my little boys to Jesus! Each time one of my children made the decision to follow Jesus, I was reminded of the incredible privilege God had given me of not only giving physical life to these precious souls but also of teaching them about and leading them to the One who could give them freedom from sin and eternal life forever in heaven.

Charles & Me

Joy filled our hearts, as we discovered in June that God had blessed us with another baby, due to arrive in March of 2014! After suffering the miscarriage in early May, I was a bit apprehensive and tried to alleviate all extra stress that might endanger the baby. Throughout the next few months, it became evident that my body and emotions were worn out as I struggled through a tough pregnancy. All the emotional trauma I had been through caught up with me as well. I had a horrible fear of more angry outbursts and invasions of privacy. As the baby's due date drew closer, my midwife realized that something was not right with the baby's position, so she scheduled an ultrasound. As we watched, the technician showed us that our baby (a boy!), almost two weeks from my due date, was already measuring a week overdue and was in a transverse position. Due to his size she could not tell where the umbilical cord was or if it was part of the problem or not. My body had already been playing with labor for a couple of days, and the situation needed to be resolved. After going home and quickly packing everyone up, we headed to Warsaw so the children could stay with my family while we were at the hospital.

That early March morning dawned cold, yet sunny and bright. As we registered at the hospital, I was very nervous. Never had I been in a situation like this, where the baby did not just come on its own. The next few hours were agony as the doctor tried numerous times to turn the baby. They gave me Pitocin while also partially prepping me for a cesarean. In the early evening, things went south when my placenta began to abrupt. Within minutes we were headed to surgery. The Lord blessed me with a very sweet, soft-spoken, and kind doctor, who was exactly what I needed at that point. I had never felt so worn out and "done" before. Things moved quickly, and before long I could hear the doctor and nurses working to deliver my baby. I kept fading in and out, and a nurse kept trying to keep me conscious. I will never forget hearing the doctor say, "She never would have made it through a normal delivery."

I knew then that God had used the placental abruption to save both my baby's life and mine.

After untangling the baby from his umbilical cord, which turned out to be wrapped all around him, the doctor held up Caleb Edward for me to see. I wept when I heard his loud, unhappy cry. My heart broke that I could not hold him, but they put his face close to mine. As I talked softly to him, he opened his eyes and stopped crying. As soon as they moved him away from me, he would start up again. After several times of this happening, the nurse figured out he just wanted his mommy!

When I was finally moved to the recovery room for observation, they brought Caleb to me, and I could finally hold my precious son. He looked like Samuel's twin, at birth, which amazed me. Charles and I prayed over him, as we had with each of our children after the birth, dedicating him to the Lord. We thanked God for His protection, mercy, and deliverance from a situation that could have turned out very differently. Caleb was the name of a man in the Bible who was willing to stand alone with Joshua against the entire nation of Israel, encouraging them to trust and obey God. We prayed that our little boy would have that same level of commitment to following and obeying God. He was also named for my maternal grandfather, Edward.

Caleb at birth

The next few months were hard since I had a lot of healing to do. My body did not handle the stress of the induced labor and emergency surgery very well. I almost had to go back into the hospital because of fluid building up around my heart. I am so thankful that my family let us live with them for a couple of weeks while I tried to heal. Caleb was a very fussy baby at night, which resulted in very low amounts of sleep. One of my younger sisters was such a blessing during those times. She would take Caleb in between feedings so that I could get a little sleep. That helped so much! Everyone in the family pitched in, helping in every realm of life especially with the other kids and trying to ensure as speedy a recovery as possible.

We found out later that Caleb's head had been wedged in my hip for such a long time that the plates of his skull were severely overlapped. After many trips to our chiropractor, he became a much happier baby. His strong-willed nature became very apparent early on, and Charles and I wondered what we had done in naming him Caleb. But we decided that all that stubbornness was a special gift from God because Caleb in the Bible must have been a stubborn person, too, to stand against the whole nation of Israel. So, as we began working with our youngest son, who had more energy and determination than any of his big brothers, we asked God to make him into a man who would be willing to stand for what was right against the crowd.

He was a cuddly little guy right from the beginning, though, and very much loved being my baby boy—a position he is still very proud to hold.

When we met with the doctor for our follow-up visit, he informed me that my uterus had become thin and had no muscles left around it. He strongly advised us to be "done" with having children. Our midwife also informed us that she would not take me as a patient if it was not at least a year before I got pregnant again. She knew that my body had reached the point of requiring a long rest period.

When I look back at those doctor visits, I have to thank the Lord, realizing how He intervened for me at a very crucial time. Having babies was my dream come true, but I knew my midwife was right, and given the trauma of Caleb's birth, I wondered if the doctor was too. My heart was so grateful to hear Charles agree to the conditions laid down by the midwife, and though he was not thrilled with the decision, I told him, I had to have a time to rest and heal.

God knew that during those next fifteen months or so, our lives would be extra crazy as He led us up mountains and through valleys and into the new ministry, He had for us. I am so grateful for the way God used wise medical advisors to help direct in my husband's heart.

The Lord blessed us allowing Charles to ordained by my father's church in April 2014.

Charles' Ordination - Spring 2014

Throughout that summer and fall, we checked into a couple of churches out of state that were looking for a pastor. We quickly fell in love with one of them, and from all appearances (and we believed because of many answers to prayer), it was where the Lord was directing and moving us. In fact, God was using the whole situation to direct and move us—just not in the way we imagined. Our hearts were completely devastated when we received the phone call informing us that the door to that ministry was closed. God had put us in a position of being prostrate before Him again. In 2013, some weeks after Charles' resignation, I had asked him if he had prayed about our going somewhere in Africa as missionaries. He had told me that he was very open to it if God led that way. That night, as another ministry door that had appeared so open was clearly shut by the Lord, we looked at each other with the same realization—the increasing burden for Africa that God had placed in Charles' heart over many years was no accident. In recent months, we both had become increasingly burdened for the need of missionaries to bring in the harvest of souls in Cameroon, West Africa, and had been praying together that God would send more missionaries there to help. We did not realize we were praying for God to send us.

The next couple of months, we prayed, and Charles contacted his veteran missionary friend, who had been in Cameroon for well over two decades, to find out about the possibility of making a survey trip. We found it hard to believe all that God did during those months because it felt like doors began opening like a flood as we prepared for our journey to the Dark Continent. I really wanted to take Daniel and Charles Jr. with us on the trip to see what their reactions would be. I knew if they got excited about what God wanted for our family, the younger children would be excited too. But the money was not there. We began to pray that the Lord would make a way, and He did! Before it was over, Charles' contact at Golden Rule had gotten round trip tickets for all four of us, that would take us to Kenya, South Africa, and Cameroon for roughly the same price that would normally have covered only two of us going to Cameroon. God was so good, and we were so excited! The hardest part of the adventure for me was leaving my five younger children for over a month, but Charles and I got to build strong relationships with our two older children during those weeks in Africa together, which was invaluable.

There were so many ways God provided funds and worked out details that it made us sit back in wonder. I remember Charles saying numerous times, "It's like God is our personal travel agent!"

6

THE CALL TO THE HARVEST

We flew out of O'Hare Airport the evening of April 6, 2015, headed for Kenya, East Africa. After a layover in Amsterdam and a second flight, we arrived safely in Nairobi, where we were met by a veteran missionary from a city nearby. The few days we spent with him and his sweet family will always hold some of my most treasured memories as we got to see a small piece of Kenya and the missionary work there. I will never be able to forget the precious children we met playing in the village one day. They were so sweet, their smiles contagious, and their precious, open hearts, wanting to be loved, stole a part of my heart that day. As our short time there came to a close and our plane left the ground, headed for South Africa, I wept. God broke my heart anew for the need of laborers in His harvest fields.

By the time we reached South Africa, I was very excited. The missionaries we were going to visit there had been friends of mine for a long time, and I loved them dearly. They had told us ahead of time that we would be actively involved in working with their children's outreaches while we were there, and I had already prepared many lessons, crafts, and activities. I was so excited to be able to teach little ones again! Though there were fun hours spent shopping for gifts to bring home to family and friends, my fondest memories will always be the hours spent with the children and young people in the ministries in South Africa. Both Charles and I felt so fulfilled and happy during those days, and Daniel and Charles Jr. enjoyed it very much too.

When the day arrived for us to leave South Africa, I told Charles that a part of my heart had now been left behind in two African countries, and now what was left of it was going to Cameroon. He laughed and said he knew the feeling.

Late that night, after a long flight, we arrived in Douala, the largest city and commercial center of Cameroon. The heat and humidity were stifling as we got off the plane, entered the airport, and went through the paperwork to be allowed into the country. The veteran missionary with whom Charles was friends was there to greet us, and we all went to a place he had secured for us to spend the night. It was not the best night of sleep we had ever had because Charles and I had to share a twin bed. In 100-degree temperatures, that is just a little too close!

Charles showing a young man how the accordion worked in Cameroon

The next day, our missionary friend took us in his small plane an hour north to the Northwest Region of Cameroon to the village of Sabga, where he and his family lived and where his runway and airplane hangar were. The flight was cramped since Daniel, Charles Jr., and I sat in the back with the luggage. Thanks to headphones, I could hear what was being said in the front of the plane. As we flew over multiple villages in French-speaking areas, the missionary talked about the desperate need for missionaries to reach so many places where the gospel had never gone. I remember hearing his voice crack as the love he had for those people caused tears to come. I looked out the airplane windows and saw the roofs of little huts in those villages and prayed, "God, what can we do to help these people hear of You and Your love for them?"

After we landed and had some breakfast, we all headed to church because it was Sunday morning. The singing that filled that crowded church that morning will always ring in my ears. It was beautiful. I remember we sang, "Surely goodness and mercy shall follow me all the days, all the days of my life."

The next few days would involve great deal of learning for us because missionary family camp began the following evening. That allowed us to spend a lot of time getting to know the other missionaries from various places in Cameroon. They had gathered at the veteran missionary's homestead for a time of preaching, fellowship, and relaxation. Those days were sweet. A pastor from the States taught multiple sessions on walking with God. We never could have dreamed he would later be one of our supporting pastors as well as one of the men who would help send us off at our commissioning service and then the one who would preach for Charles' funeral. His wife also taught a few ladies' sessions throughout the family camp, and those days were encouraging for all of us.

That first evening of camp, we met Ben and Becca Sinclair and their children for the first time. They were working tirelessly to make grilled pizzas for everyone there. It was fascinating to watch them work as a team, and the pizzas were phenomenal.

Ben and Becca invited us to come to their home in Bambili that following weekend to be involved in the church services of the two churches they had planted in that area. In the diary I kept during our survey trip, "I wrote concerning our time with the Sinclairs those few days:

We went to church here in Bambili this morning and heard Brother Paul teach a wonderful Sunday school lesson from Joshua 7 about making sure we are seeking the Lord above all things, keeping our heart right with God, and not hiding sin. Then I played the piano for the song service, and the boys and I sang, "There Is a Happy Land." Charles preached his message on the life and childhood of Jesus. We also had the Lord's Supper. That was a sweet time to celebrate and remember our Lord with believers in Cameroon and to realize again the sweetness of being a part of the body of Christ!

After the church service and a quick bathroom stop, we headed to Faith Baptist in Bamenda. They were in the middle of the song time when we arrived. Charles preached on heaven, and we sang again. The church was packed, and it was a blessed experience to share the Lord's Supper again with another group of believers. Charles enjoyed getting to visit with Timothy, a young man in the Bible Institute."

Charles would never preach in those churches again. God gave him only one Sunday with each group of people before his death. But on that trip, he got to do in Cameroon what made him happy and fulfilled—teaching God's Word!

Survey trip - 2015

The rest of our survey trip was filled with Charles traveling into the Akwaya region with the veteran missionary, trying to soak up everything he could about what life and ministry looked like in Cameroon. I loved getting to cook from scratch and thoroughly enjoyed being able to work in the kitchen. Unfortunately, Charles Jr. and I got very sick the last half of our trip. He recovered much quicker, but it took days before I felt even partway normal.

There were tears as we flew out of Cameroon. There was no doubt in Charles' mind that this was where God wanted us. I, too, knew it was where God wanted us even though part of me felt scared of all the unknowns that lay ahead. God had given us a love for the people, a burden to see them reached with the gospel. We could hear Him calling, "Who will go for us?"

Charles preaching in Cameroon

Within a few days of our return from Cameroon, Charles and all the children were deathly sick in bed with the same virus I had been hit with in Cameroon. For almost a week I was the only one able to be out of bed. I was kept crazy busy, taking care of Charles and the kids as their bodies fought off that awful bug. One day, in the midst of feeling completely overwhelmed, I walked into our bedroom and told Charles, who was lying there miserable, that I firmly believed that this sickness was God's sign to us that we were *not* supposed to go

Cameroon as missionaries! Even being sick, Charles did not miss a beat. He quickly retorted that it was quite to the contrary; this was God confirming we were supposed to go. The devil was just trying to discourage me.

Over the coming months, as we moved forward with the many details that were involved in preparing to start deputation (from having prayer cards printed and designing a website to meeting with our prospective mission board, from formulating a list of churches for possible meetings to looking for a motorhome in which to travel as a family) I would find myself crippled with fear—fear of the unknown, fear of deputation, fear of being completely incapable of being a good enough missionary as well as a wife and mother, and more than anything else, the fear of losing a child on the mission field. As I battled in my heart, knowing that we were doing what God had planned for us but afraid of so many things all at once, turmoil and guilt would overwhelm me. I felt like I was letting Charles down over and over again because his excitement never wavered. God heard my heart cries when I begged Him for deliverance and freedom from my fears. In August, while we were attending the Christ Life Conference, God answered my prayers. An evangelist friend preached a message on King David's mighty men. I do not remember all of what he said, but I know that while he was preaching, the Lord spoke to my heart, reminding me that I was right. I was incapable of being a missionary, protecting my kids from harm, or doing anything useful on my own. It was going to be Him! He would be the missionary through me; He would be the protection; He would be the one accomplishing the work and doing amazing things throughout deputation and in Cameroon. As the Lord brought me to surrender and flooded my heart with peace and freedom from fear, my excitement about the unknowns of the journey ahead was clearly coming from Him.

God answered a multitude of prayers in that we were accepted by First Light Baptist Missions, found an affordable motorhome that was perfect for our needs, and meetings started being scheduled. In mid-October, we were thrilled with the wonderful news that God was blessing our family with another precious baby, due to arrive in June of 2016. Stephy, who had been earnestly praying for a baby sister for months, was so excited and immediately certain that God had answered her prayers. She immediately began praying that her little sister would have blond hair, blue eyes, a strong heart, and "lungs that wouldn't crack"! Thanks to a midwife who knew of ways to quickly boost my hormone levels, I did not miscarry again, and we pressed forward, preparing for deputation travels to begin, the first Sunday in November of 2015.

7

FINDING GOD FAITHFUL

*C*harles and I spent hours preparing for that new chapter of our lives and ministry to begin, but we never would have dreamed that it would be the final chapter of life and ministry we would do together. Looking back on those days, weeks, months, and years we spent traveling around to multiple states, sharing the burden and calling God had placed on our hearts for the people of Cameroon, I am so thankful for the numerous sweet moments we shared together as a family. As we drove thousands of miles, there were many times of serious talk, prayer together, uncontrollable laughter, jokes from the last church being repeated a thousand times, lots of long naps, new songs being learned, school being done, stories listened to, and most of all, lots of dreaming about our future life in Cameroon.

One of our first meetings was at the church where Charles had spent the majority of his growing up years and where we had been married eleven years earlier. There was so much joy and excitement, and many prayers for God's leading and desires of the heart were fulfilled during the months of deputation that followed. Our first few months involved mission conferences and meetings in Indiana,

Wisconsin, Ohio, and Michigan. Every time we heard about a new supporting church, there were cheers and prayers of thankfulness!

Charles' quoting from memory the Bible book of Jonah

Charles had a great burden to see our children actively involved in the deputation ministry and process. He did not want them to feel like they were just being dragged along for the ride; he wanted them to see firsthand how God could use each of them and to experience the joys and blessings that come with serving Him. I had taught them multiple songs to sing together for special numbers. In addition, the older boys had prepared some violin solos and duets to play. Charles also had asked Luke Hicks, whom he dearly loved and had taught during his years with the Bible institute, to give the older boys lessons in chalk drawing throughout the summer preceding deputation.

While Charles was preaching, the boys would draw a picture that went along with the message. Though they had multiple chalk talk drawings, the two they did the most were the ones that went along with Charles' message about the Samaritan woman at the well in John 4 and a Cameroonian village picture that went along Charles' sermon on living for eternity. I never would have dreamed that the points from those two messages that I heard week after week for over two years would become the foundation and purpose that would keep me from falling apart and losing focus after Charles' death.

The boys finishing a chalk drawing during deputation

The first eight months of deputation went as smoothly as we could have possibly imagined, with only the typical kinds of hiccups anyone has when living in a motorhome on the road. We found out that the baby we looked forward to meeting in June was a girl. The gracious technician rechecked multiple times for me because I had a hard time believing that we could possibly be having another girl. But it was true, and Stephy Joy calmly informed me, "Mommy, I told you it was a girl. Jesus answered my prayers!"

We had finished our first extended deputation trip out East, and there was a lot of excitement in the air as we awaited the soon arrival of our baby girl. She decided to come on her own schedule, which meant a week late. I woke up early the morning of June 22 to my water breaking. I expected labor to start, but it did not. Due to my cesarean with Caleb, the situation was a bit more complicated. My midwife advised trying castor oil to help get labor going, and it definitely did the trick. Within a few hours, I was in consistent labor, but it was very different than any of my previous labors, proving to be more painful, more intense, and with even more back labor than normal. I would find out during the delivery that my little girl was posterior, which was one of the main reasons for the extra discomfort. The wee hours of the morning of June 23 found us rushing toward the birthing center as labor intensified. As we drove, I told Charles I thought my water was breaking, gushing over and over again. When we arrived at the birthing center, Charles and the nurse helped me get into the wheelchair. They saw what I did not see—lots of blood. My midwife had not arrived yet, but the backup midwife and the nurse quickly hooked me up to a stress monitor to check on the baby. Her heart-rate was good. Though I did not understand everything going on, I knew that I was quickly wearing out and could tell my midwife was a little anxious. Pepsi was forced down my throat, and my midwife gave me a shot to help ease the pain and cause me to relax. Those last thirty minutes before Emmeline Hope was born are a blur to me. I seriously believed I was going to die giving birth to her. All I remember from the end is my midwife locking her eyes with mine and saying, "Stephanie, you are going to get this baby out on the next push!"

As I cried out to God for strength, I gave the last bit of energy I had left, and my precious baby girl was born. I saw her flipped over, my midwife moving with lightning speed, a tube going down my baby's throat, an oxygen mask. I heard my midwife saying, "Come on, baby girl!"

I knew something was seriously wrong. My baby would not breathe and was completely non-responsive. They rushed her out of the room as the team worked on her, leaving me lying there on the bed alone. Never before in my life had I felt so entirely weak and helpless. I lay there, crying out and telling God He could not take my baby girl. Immediately, conviction filled my heart because I knew that that precious baby was not mine but His. I found myself surrendering my baby over to Him again, begging Him to have mercy and spare the life of Emmeline Hope. I had loved her name for several years, hoping I would have another little girl and the chance to use it. Her name means "work of confident expectation." Indeed, through her birth, God did just that in our hearts.

Our new family of ten with baby Emmeline - 2016

A half-hour passed before I heard her scream, and then she screamed for the next hour straight. We discovered her jaw had been dislocated, and as a result, she could not even close her mouth. All the drugs that had been pumped into her had to wear off. I was so thankful for a local chiropractor, who came six hours after her birth and adjusted her. She relaxed significantly after the adjustment, and I began to breathe a little easier. My parents brought our other children to the birthing center to meet their little sister. We spent time thanking God for sparing our precious baby girl's life, and everyone took turns holding her. Looking back, I have no regrets for every moment spent cuddling my big baby girl, who weighed nine pounds and five ounces when she was born. She was one of the sweetest, calmest babies God gave us, hardly ever crying and very content wherever she was. It was as if God had perfectly designed her for deputation! Since she spent 90 percent of her first years in the motorhome, she viewed that as home and would almost get scared when we got back to our house after a long time away. She would return to being totally happy when taken back out to her little bed.

Emmy Hope looked nothing like her big sister and definitely showed signs of favoring mommy in the looks department, which continued to be the case as she got older. Within a couple of months, her dimpled smile, curly blond hair, and beautiful blue eyes were melting hearts and winning affection at every church we were in.

Deputation travel became even crazier with eight children and all the extra baby gear that now accompanied us. We loved it, though, and I spent many hours on the road cuddling Emmy or Emmy and Caleb at the same time. Caleb really struggled with losing his position as the baby in the family, but he eventually relaxed as I constantly assured him that he was my baby boy. He loved to cuddle; so many times, both arms would be full, holding my two sleeping babies.

To Die Is Gain

In our camper with Caleb and Emmeline

Mid-October found us home for three days in the middle of a busy mission conference season, and I had a long list of things to do in the few days we were to be there. But on the second day I slipped and fell down our basement stairs while holding Emmeline, three and a half months old at the time. Praise the Lord, she was not injured at all, but due to not being able to catch myself in any way as I fell, I ended up with a fractured ankle. Six weeks in a boot and on crutches in a motorhome as we travelled from church to church was not the version of "adventure" I had pictured for the Fall months, but I asked the Lord to give me a token of good and to show me His purpose for this trial. A couple of weeks later in family devotions, we read the children a story about a missionary in Africa. It included a gospel presentation using the wordless book. Through that, the Lord answered our prayers and opened Stephy Joy's eyes to her need of a Savior. She finally realized that her heart was black with sin and that she needed Jesus to make it white. Again, tears flowed as I listened to my precious daughter ask Jesus to forgive her sins and give her a clean heart. God gave me my "token for good" amid the inconvenience of a fractured ankle!

Our second ministry picture

After a few more crazy weeks on the road, we were home in December and very excited about the Christmas season. I was finally out of my boot and only had to wear a brace. Getting a family picture for Christmas every year was a tradition we started the year Daniel was born, but Charles had told me this would be the last year we would be able to afford it. I had figured out coordinating outfits for our family and scheduled a photo shoot at a local studio. That cold, snowy December morning, exactly two months after I had broken my ankle, we were busy loading the kids in the van. I was in a hurry because we were running a little behind, and as I came down our sloping driveway, I slipped on ice under the snow, fell backwards, and caught myself with my left wrist. I asked Charles to grab a couple of ibuprofens and my Ace bandages. I wrapped my wrist up and took the pills, hoping it was just a bad sprain. The photo shoot became a torture session as pain shot through my hand, wrist, and arm, making me want to vomit, but the good pictures we got that day are treasured mementoes for me.

By the following morning, we determined that it was definitely more than a sprain, and Charles drove me to the orthopedist. The x-ray completed, I waited in the room for the doctor. As she walked into the room, the first words out of her mouth were, "What pain meds are you on right now?"

I told her I had taken a couple of acetaminophen and ibuprofen tablets the day before. She proceeded to repeat her question and told me she did not understand how I had gone twenty-four hours without them, given the condition my wrist was in. When she showed me the x-ray, I asked, "What is that broken-up mountain range?"

She exclaimed, "That's your wrist. It's shattered!"

That was not the news I was hoping to hear that morning, and my mind reeled as I waited for the cast to be put on. Eight children, deputation, and a shattered wrist—how were these three things supposed to coincide? Again, I went to the Lord, asking Him to bring beauty out of ashes and show me the "good" in the midst of this new trial. Within a few days, He answered that prayer when my sweet four-year old Samuel approached me one morning, telling me that he needed to get saved. I was concerned about making sure that his interest was sincere and not something being forced on him by his big sister, who had been daily preaching to him since she got saved. So, I told Samuel to mention it to Daddy after family devotions that evening. He followed through and went over to Charles as soon as devotions were over, telling him he needed to be saved. Charles spent time going over the gospel with him, and it was clear that he understood. And that night, another one of our precious children joined the family of God!

The rest of December was filled with fun Christmas activities even though the pain level in my wrist kept increasing. Being unable to play the piano was hard, especially during the Christmas season, since I loved to relax at the piano in the evening under the twinkling lights by playing Christmas carols and songs. But I was so thankful to be able to spend that holiday season with my family and all eight of my precious children. I kept reminding myself how good God had been to me that year.

January of 2017 found me back at the doctor's office in horrific pain. I was told that the bone in my wrist had deteriorated and needed surgery immediately. I felt bad because that meant Charles had to cancel meetings and completely readjust his schedule. As always, members of my family, along with the Hicks, were there to help with the children when we headed to the hospital two days later for the surgery. God was so good, and though the pain afterwards was way worse than I was expecting, the surgery was a success, and my wrist was put back together with a plate and multiple screws.

The next few months of deputation were a bit stressful as we had to plan around multiple physical therapy appointments. I learned to function with a virtually useless wrist for several months. It was a happy day when I was given permission to start playing the piano again. Little by little mobility improved, and by late spring, I had almost completely recovered. I was thankful to be able to function normally again, realizing how much I had taken that gift for granted.

The rest of 2017 was full of craziness with deputation in full swing as we pressed forward toward the finish line. Life in the motorhome was always full of noise and activity, but those days drew us very close as a family. When you are living within a couple of feet of another person every single moment of the day and night, you have to become best friends. God was good, and the support level kept climbing, bringing much joy and excitement to our hearts. We watched the Lord meet needs and answer specific prayers. Charles began hoping that we could leave for the field by Spring of the following year.

December brought us news of another reward from the Lord and more changes to our plans. The new baby was due around Charles' birthday in August of 2018! We both were very excited at the prospect of another child; although, I dealt with a lot of fear and apprehension at the thought of the birth and delivery. But within a week of finding out I was pregnant, I started showing signs of miscarrying, and my next pregnancy test was negative. My heart broke as we travelled that day to our meeting in Wisconsin. Physical and emotional pain filled me, and I cried in the service that night as my children sang a song, they had sung many times during our two years of deputation. It had often spoken to my heart, but that evening, it ministered in a whole new way as the Lord comforted me through its words.

The Name of the Lord

To Die Is Gain

The Lord is my Shepherd, my Keeper, my Guide.
He leads me to pastures of rest;
Beside the still waters He quiets my soul,
I trust Him for His will is best.

Chorus:
The name of the Lord is a tower of strength,
A refuge of safety from harm;
The righteous run into the name of the Lord,
The name of the Lord, in confidence, free from alarm.

The Lord is my Comfort in times of distress
As suddenly life falls apart;
When [I'm] crushed by the trials that tempt me to doubt,
He whispers His love to my heart.
He whispers His love to my heart.

Chorus

The Lord is my Peace in the midst of the storm,
A haven of calm deep inside,
Imparting His strength to my weak fainting heart,
His life and His peace to abide.

Chorus

The name of the Lord is a tower of strength,
A refuge of safety from harm;
The righteous run into the name of the Lord,
The name of the Lord, in confidence, free from alarm.

—John and Mary Lynn Van Gelderen, used by permission
© 2016

Oh, if I had known that a year from then I would be trying to simply breathe and live from day to day, the words of that song would have meant even more to me!

The next month was full of emotional highs and lows as my body kept giving mixed messages, which finally resulted in our going in for an ultrasound. Though they found no heartbeat, they found evidence of a pregnancy and told me to wait a few weeks until they would be able to find the heartbeat. Over the next couple of weeks, as several of my children began showing signs of what we would later find out was whooping cough, I struggled with knowing that something was not right with the pregnancy. The first week of January of 2018, I went into early labor and had to work through the emotions throughout the day of realizing that my baby was indeed with Jesus. Late that night, after several hours of heavy labor, our sweet Rose was born. Many tears were shed, but then peace and comfort filled my heart, knowing my Savior had done all things well. Rose was not developed normally and would not have lived, and God in His love and mercy, took her to Himself early, where she could bloom, beautiful and perfect, in Heaven. Later that year after Charles died, I found comfort in knowing that he was welcomed to Heaven by our children who were already there.

The same week I miscarried, the doctor confirmed that our family had whooping cough, and we got to spend a week at home together while the medicine did its work and we tried to heal and recover. Those days found us busily packing and purging as we prepared to move out of the house that we had called home for thirteen years. In the Lord's providence, the week before we were scheduled to sign with a realtor to sell our house, some friends of ours called to say that they wanted to buy it. We were so thankful for the money it saved both families and for the Lord's provision of a buyer so quickly.

In February we moved out of our house in Mishawaka and into a rented farmhouse that belonged to an older couple in our church. The plan was to live there for a few months before heading to Cameroon in August. Deputation continued as we asked the Lord to bring the remaining support we needed.

As March progressed, I started feeling very strange, dealing with dizziness, a foggy brain, headaches, and extreme fatigue. After going to the doctor, I found out I was battling worn adrenals and the Epstein- Barr virus. It would be months before I would feel like a normal person again. God used those days of sickness to draw me closer to Him in new ways, because some days I felt like I was losing my mind. Some days I was so weak that I could barely even get out of bed in the motorhome to care for my family. I had to force myself to get everyone ready for church on Sundays. Charles was an amazing husband during those days, doing all he could to try to make it possible to let me rest in peace and quiet, since he came to realize that was the only way for my body to heal. God drew us very close together during those months, and I saw in a whole new way how much he loved me. He saw in a new way that I was truly committed to going to Cameroon no matter what.

The rental home in Warsaw was a great blessing to us that year. It was a comfortable place to live, and the children loved living on a farm with sheep and cows to see every day. They had so much fun riding their little four-wheeler up and down the long driveway and playing outside. Cornfields surrounded the house, and the view was beautiful. During our time there, we prepared and shipped out the last trailer load of barrels and totes full of our belongings and supplies for overseas. We also finished packing up all but the last few pieces of luggage that would go with us on the plane.

One Wednesday evening, late that summer, we had gotten home from prayer meeting, put all the children to bed, and were preparing for bed ourselves, when four-year old Caleb came into our bedroom. He did not have his typical ornery smile, but instead was very serious. He told me he needed to get saved. I started talking with him and soon realized he understood and was not playing with me. Charles also asked him questions, and before too much time had passed, together we got to listen to our youngest son ask Jesus to save him from his sins. His words weren't fancy, but his childlike faith was beautiful. I'll always treasure the memories of that evening. I realize now it was such a special gift from the Lord that both of us were there to get to lead him to Jesus!

The first week of August, we made a last-minute decision to drive up to Michigan for the Christ Life Conference. It had become a very special week for our family, and we were so excited to spend just a little time with people who had become very dear to us. I will always thank the Lord for the teaching and preaching we heard at those conferences. God used so many of those messages to change us more into His image. Because of the clear teaching from the different preachers, Charles' eyes were opened in deeper ways to the truths of "Christ in you, the hope of glory." He lived in a constant state of wanting to know Christ more. Those last few months of marriage were some of our sweetest as we sought together to know our Savior in deeper ways than ever before. It was in those last couple of months before leaving for Cameroon, that the Lord brought Charles to the firm conviction that He was going to bring revival to all of Cameroon. I'll never forget Charles' excitement about that. He would talk about it, as if it were already happening. God had given him a vision of what He wanted to do in the country we loved so much.

Our church held the commissioning service for us a couple weeks later, and we were privileged to have two pastors from supporting churches join us for the day, as well as having Bro. Don Stertz from Wyldewood Baptist Church, the home of our mission board, preach the main message. It was a day of rejoicing, tears, and prayer as our pastor, the deacons, and other men of the church, gathered around our family, and committed us to God. The song our family sang together for the service communicated our commitment to obeying and following the command of our God.

Woe Is unto Me

Every people, from every nation, need to hear the truth.
Who will tell them, of the Savior? Is God calling you?
Thousands are dying everyday now, with no hope or light.

How can we stand by without telling of Christ's great
    sacrifice?

Woe is unto me if I preach not the gospel!
Only Christ can set men free from their sin for all eternity.
Who will go for the Lord? Who will preach His Word?
Who will tell the nations that Jesus Christ is Lord?

We have family, we have neighbors, who do not know
    Christ.
Time is short now, and we must tell them of eternal life.
They need Jesus, their sins forgiven, a change in their lives.
For without Him, they are dying, with no hope in sight.

Woe is unto me if I preach not the gospel!
Only Christ can set men free from their sin for all eternity.
We must go for the Lord! We must preach His Word!
We must tell the nations that Jesus Christ is Lord.

—Matt Black, used by permission

Our commissioning service - 2018

During that summer Charles made several statements to me as if he knew his time on earth was short, telling me what he wanted me to do in multiple realms of life "if something ever happens."

On Samuel's sixth birthday in the middle of that September, our family was having a quiet little birthday party at our house. As we sat around the table, watching Samuel open his presents, Charles began discussing one of his favorite subjects with the children—the different crowns that are promised to believers in Scripture. He loved to quiz the children on the names of the crowns and how they could be earned. That evening the last one to be mentioned was the crown of life or the martyr's crown. I'll never forget listening to Charles talk about that crown with such desire—not a desire for death but to be found worthy of receiving that crown and to cast it at His Savior's feet. He even went so far as to say "a shot to the head" would be the easiest, most painless way to earn it. I became very upset with him as he talked about wishing for the honor of receiving that crown. I told him he had children to help raise so he couldn't die! I will never forget how he smiled at me and said happily, "Oh, Sweetie, I'll wait awhile. There is so much I want to do for the Lord in Cameroon first!"

One of our last family pictures with Charles

He did not know that in some strange, yet wonderful way, God would grant him his heart's desire less than six weeks later.

October arrived, bringing lots of excitement and many other emotions since we knew our time of departure for Cameroon was fast approaching. Looking back on that time now, I realize that if we had known our days together were almost over, Charles and I would have spent lots more time together. But we didn't know. God had filled our hearts with confidence in His leading and a peace that passed all understanding, and He had even given Charles a vision of our family starting to learn French, once we were settled on the field in case it became necessary to move into one of the French speaking regions due to the conflict in the English speaking regions.

Our last day before flying out was intense because we had to pack, unpack, and repack, trying to make all the weight even out among the different suitcases. I was so thankful for my mother's help that day. She worked her packing magic and made it all work out in the end. My grandparents came over that evening, and we had a very special season of prayer together. It was the last time they would ever see Charles on this earth.

On Wednesday, October 17, 2018, we did the final packing of our luggage and then had to go through the tearful process of saying goodbye to family and friends. Our hearts were filled with anticipation and excitement but also sadness at leaving behind so many people we loved so dearly.

The words of Jesus kept ringing in my ears that day: "Whosoever will come after me, let him deny himself, and take up his cross, and follow me. For whosoever will save his life shall lose it; but whosoever shall lose his life for my sake and the gospel's, the same shall save it" (Mark 8:34–35).

My parents drove us to the airport, and we met up with the Hicks family on the way. We had lunch together, and it was a sweet time of fellowship—one that I am sure all of us who were there will always treasure. We arrived at the airport and went through the strenuous process of checking in all our luggage. When it came time for final goodbyes, we stood there together as my father and Steve Hicks prayed, asking God for His hand of protection and blessing to go with us. Innumerable tears were shed, and as we headed toward the TSA check-in, we waved our last goodbyes, never dreaming that would be the last time any of them would see Charles on this earth.

The Lord was good to allow us to get through security and to our departure gate with no problems or complications. Before long, we found ourselves boarding the Air France flight that would take us on the first leg of our journey to our new home. As the plane left the ground, I looked out the window, thinking it would be years before I saw American soil again. The children were amazing throughout the flight, staying very content most of the time. Hours later, we landed in Paris. After the grueling process of getting through security, we made our way to our next departure gate, where we relaxed for several hours. The kids were enthralled with all the new sights, and we all felt a bit off balance, due to jet lag beginning to hit us.

Within a few hours, we boarded our second flight, which was also calm and smooth. We arrived in Yaoundé, the capital of Cameroon, on the evening of Thursday, October 18, 2018.

8

"WE'RE HOME!"

We had arrived in the land that had become home in our hearts many months before—Cameroon, West Africa! Ben Sinclair, our coworker, team leader, and dear friend, met us at the airport in Yaoundé late that Wednesday evening, and greeted us with a smile and, "Welcome home!"

I remember my heart skipped a beat when he uttered those words! We *were* home! The place where we would meet the people God had filled our hearts with love for; the place we had talked about and prayed for constantly; the place we had shipped the majority of our earthly belongings to; the place to which God had called us to serve Him, we believed, for the rest of our lives. It was the beginning of our dream come true, and there was so much excitement and thanksgiving in our hearts! That night we piled into the rented bus, which was loaded down on top and in the back with all thirty-four of our footlockers and the few suitcases we brought. We were driven to the mission house in Yaoundé, where we could catch a few hours of sleep before getting on the road early Thursday morning. Everyone went to bed quickly, but I could not sleep. The sounds of that African night could be heard over the fan in our room, and as I lay there, I cried, realizing I had said goodbye to my parents, family, and friends, and it would be years before I would see them again. The new life ahead of me was my dream come true, but knowing an ocean lay between me and many I loved was hard to swallow that night. As I lay there, the Lord brought a very important verse to my heart, and in those moments, I once again surrendered to God's will for me: "He that loveth father or mother more than me is not worthy of me: and he that loveth son or daughter more than me is not worthy of me. And he that taketh not his cross, and followeth after me, is not worthy of me" (Matthew 10:37–38).

More than anything that night, I knew that I wanted to be worthy of my Savior. I wanted to take up the cross He had for me. With that surrender came peace and joy—and a couple of hours of much-needed sleep.

We were up bright and early and got on the road headed north by 6:00 a.m. We knew we had to not only make it to our destination before curfew at 6:00 p.m. but also allow enough time for the driver to reach his destination for the night. We made a couple of stops along the way to pick up powdered milk for Emmy, a fan for our bedroom, and some drinks. When we made it to Bafoussam, we stopped at a missionary family's home for a much-needed bathroom stop and leg stretching. Mrs. B gave us egg salad sandwiches, popcorn, and carrot sticks for lunch on the road, and we were off again.

There were multiple military check points along the way, but we were very thankful that no one gave us any trouble. After hours of travel, we reached the big city of Bamenda and made our way through without complications. Oh, the joy and excitement that filled our hearts, as we arrived in the village of Bambili Friday evening after that long, hot bus ride from the capital city of Yaoundé to the North-west Region of Cameroon, where we planned to spend "the rest of our lives."

There were eleven of us: Charles, me, Daniel, Charles Jr, Joseph, Hudson Taylor, Stephy Joy, Samuel, Caleb, Emmeline, and Liberty Hicks, our good friend and helper. As we all began learning to adjust to a different lifestyle, our new normal included lots of red dirt, sweat, dirty clothes, electricity that was off more than on, many big bugs, mice running down the halls (oh wait, we had mice running around in our rental house in the United States), and cold showers (unless you remembered to heat water on the stove). We were getting used to using filtered water for everything, sleeping on mattresses on the floor, occasionally waking up to distant gun shots, and dealing with ghost town Mondays and early curfews every evening. But we loved it! God had given us complete freedom from fear and had filled our hearts and souls with peace and contentment in the life He had called us to. We were very optimistic that He was going to help us adjust to new things and give us grace to go through whatever was ahead of us in this new ministry.

Those twelve days were spent unpacking footlockers, suitcases, barrels, and totes. We had moved to Africa, and it was kind of like Christmas as things were discovered that had been sent over months before. The kids were excited to have special toys back that they had sent ahead; Daddy was excited to have tools and books ready to put to use; and Mommy was thrilled to find pots, pans, seasonings and things she needed to make good food for everyone to enjoy.

There were many moments of screams and laughter during those days as spiders, bugs, and lizards were discovered! Liberty decided that, if she wanted to have any savings left when her time with us was over, she would have to lower her payments to the boys for eliminating creepy-crawly things because they were everywhere! The funniest lizard incident took place the evening before Charles was killed, but I'm getting ahead of myself. I will share those fond memories shortly.

Our unwelcome visitors

Nothing is as tasty as fresh fruits and vegetables from the market, and I loved getting to make everything from scratch. It was an awesome adventure, and I had many ideas to try in the kitchen. Charles was determined to get us settled into our new home as quickly as possible and worked so diligently to fix things around the house, trying to stop leaking toilets, fix bad wiring, keep the bathroom water heater working, as well as interacting with men from the village. He was so happy that, with Ben Sinclair's help, he could buy me a stove, refrigerator, and freezer for our new home. They were beautiful, and the stove with five burners on top was the nicest I had ever had. Of course, voltage regulators were a necessity, and I was very thankful Charles understood how they worked because I was much slower at figuring out what could be plugged in and when.

We loved having two little children who lived in our walled compound come over to our house each day. A little girl who lived there soon became Emmy's little friend, and I envisioned them becoming friends for life. Emmy loved wearing her new friend's "slippers" (flip-flops), and she loved eating some of Emmy's food! It was a great arrangement for both of them! They learned how to communicate, and that sweet little girl was helping us learn some Pigeon English. There also was a little boy in the compound who loved to play with our toys and had the sweetest smile. They both were a dream come true since I was so burdened to reach out to the children there.

We made multiple trips into Bamenda during those days, picking up supplies and food. We were learning how to shop in the open markets. It was really fun, and I enjoyed those trips because it gave us time to talk and ask our coworkers questions about all the new things we were learning. Charles was living his dream, and I don't ever remember a time in those twelve days that he was not beaming with joy and excitement at all God was going to do.

Bamenda Market

A week after we arrived, we were invited to attend the traditional wedding of a couple in the church. It was a very special event, and we got to observe the traditions and practices of African culture and experience authentic Cameroonian food. That wedding allowed us to see several other missionary families from the area, which was really special. Though our fellowship was brief that day, I was so excited as we talked. I thought to myself that we were finally where we were supposed to be, where we belonged.

My favorite memory from that day will always be the return trip. With the Sinclair family as well as our whole family in the church bus, we enjoyed singing together all the way home. I remember thinking as we drove, "Life can't get any better than this! We are living our dream!"

Sunday, October 28, was very special. We attended the village church in Bambili for the first time. The song service will always be a special memory. We sang "Grace That Is Greater than All Our Sin." I could not have dreamed how much I would learn about what God's grace looked like in the coming week, but in those moments as we stood there singing together with our Cameroonian brothers and sisters, we rejoiced at God's goodness in fulfilling His promises of bringing us to the place where He had called us to serve Him "for the rest of our days."

Our last Sunday with Charles - on earth

After Sunday lunch, cleanup was a family effort. Water was constantly being heated on the stove for washing dishes, and between the washer, dryers, and those putting things away, that little kitchen was full of people. But we were having so much fun! There were silly songs being sung, lots of giggles and laughs, and a host of memories we will forever cherish being made.

It was a good day—a precious gift from God and a day we will always thank Him for.

Some of my best special memories from those twelve days are of our family devotions. I remember our singing together, sometimes in almost complete darkness due to having no electricity. One evening, we got distracted talking about pictures we should take to put in the next prayer letter. The kids had some crazy ideas, which led to lots of laughter, and Charles had to round us all up and get our thoughts back on track!

The evening of Monday, October 29, will always be full of special memories. The electricity was off, so we had devotions by flashlight. Though I can't remember anything about the topic, I do remember it was a very special time together—praying, singing, and listening to Charles read Scripture. Everyone went to their rooms to get ready for bed, and we were close to shutting down for the night when a scream came from the girls' bathroom! Liberty began calling for one of the boys to come quickly, and so began the funniest adventure of our time in Cameroon!

There was a lizard in the bathroom, and it was completely freaking her out! She was willing to pay to have it removed from the bathroom and exterminated. From the safety of her bed, she was quick to offer monetary rewards to whoever would rescue her from the savage beast. I mean, lizard! A couple of the boys were courageous and went into the bathroom to commence the rescue operation, but things got ugly when the lizard slipped out of the bathroom and started running between our feet. Caleb, who was elated at the prospect of a lizard for a pet, dove for the poor creature and caught it by the tail, which tore off its body. Then the screaming got louder since there was now a tail squirming as well as a lizard running around our feet! At this point, Stephy Joy, who was horrified that this creature had invaded her room, began threatening her brothers from the safety of her bed that if the lizard got into her footlocker (her clothes), she would spit on them. Things were getting ugly! But then Caleb came to the rescue when, on his second dive, he caught the poor reptile! There were shouts of joy and relief, and then the laughter commenced. Caleb wanted a house for his new pet and decided that Mommy's huge cooking pot (which I hadn't even had a chance to use yet) would make the perfect lizard home. I think we all went to bed that night laughing, picturing what the neighbors must have thought of those crazy American missionaries, losing it over a lizard!

Our lizard visitor

9

TO DIE IS GAIN

As I come to this part of my story, I need to be very honest. Writing about the events of the day Charles was shot is one of the most painful things I have ever had to do. I have dreaded putting on paper this nightmare that still haunts me. Everything in me wants to rewind and change the plans God had for that day. But I cannot. A verse that quickly became a life support verse in the afternoon of that fateful day comes to mind: "We know that all things work together for good to them that love God, to them who are the called according to his purpose" (Romans 8:28). God's purposes in all that transpired that day are becoming clearer and yet are still, for the most part, only seen through the eye of faith. But because God's Word is true, I know that He will take all the horror and trauma He allowed that day and work it together for good.

Missionaries have always been my heroes. From the time I was a child, they were the ones I looked up to as examples to follow. Much of my free time was spent reading biographies of men and women who were completely sold out and surrendered to serving God on the mission field. Among my favorites were Gladys Aylward, Amy Carmichael, David Brainerd, Adoniram and Ann Judson, Jonathan and Rosalind Goforth, and Hudson Taylor, to mention just a few. But

To Die Is Gain

John and Betty Stam, Jim Elliot, Nate Saint, Ed McCully, Pete Fleming, and Roger Youderian were among my top heroes—not because they were worthier of admiration than the others but because they were martyrs who willingly laid down their lives, slain by the very people they loved and longed to reach with the good news of the gospel. But as I thought about going to the mission field myself, I remember wondering many times how Elisabeth Elliot and the other wives of those men could love the very people who murdered their husbands. There could be no love that strong! "But things like that don't happen now," I remember thinking, so relieved. Tuesday morning of October 30, 2018, I would find out that I was wrong.

The morning dawned beautiful, sunny, and promising. Charles had big plans with the boys for making homemade bread to take to all the neighbors as an opportunity to get to know and begin reaching out to them. Lil Charles was helping Daddy try to figure out how to run the mill and Bosch mixer off our little generator. It got a bit frustrating for Charles when he discovered there was not quite enough generator power to do everything at once like he could in the States. My husband loved to work in the kitchen and loved cooking, something I was so grateful for. Making bread was one of his all-time favorite activities, and he had gone to a lot of trouble to ship to Cameroon a grinder and a mixer plus wheat berries, cinnamon, raisins, honey, dough enhancer, yeast, and enough loaf pans to last a lifetime. His philosophy was that we could live on his bread if need be, and it was a great way to minister to people. His plan for the next few days was to turn our house into a bakery. Being the caring husband, he was, though, he let me get a load of laundry washed first that morning, since we had a huge pile up of dirty clothes because the electricity had been off. As a result, he never got the bread baking process completely underway.

That morning, I decided to try my hand at corn bread in our new oven. The oven had no temperature markings, so I had to guess what the temperature was by feeling the heat. Liberty got better internet on her phone, so she began the search for a good corn bread recipe, and she found one that sounded delicious and that we had all the ingredients for. It turned out great, and I was so happy I had discovered where 350 degrees was on the oven. We gathered around our table for what would be our last meal together as a family. I had brought maple syrup with us, and it was a very special treat with the corn bread. After breakfast, Charles said what would be the last words I remember him saying specifically to me. He thanked me for the corn bread and said it was the best he had ever had. That made me so happy, and it still makes me smile to know that Charles loved the last meal I made him.

The plans for the day changed as the morning progressed when Ben and Charles discussed the dangers that would be associated with their original plan of going to the city of Kumbo with some of the Cameroonian Christians. Due to the unrest, they decided to postpone their outreach trip and make Tuesday our market day in Bamenda. It was a much safer plan, they agreed, and they could wait to go to Kumbo another day when things were a little calmer there. Charles told me about the change of plans, and I began gathering up market bags as well as finalizing my shopping list. As always, there was discussion as to which child would get to go on the trip, and Hudson was elated to be next up for a shopping adventure. As we headed out the door, though, Charles changed his mind and said Hudson could go another time, and that he wanted Charles Jr. to go this time. Of course, that made Charles Jr. quite happy, and after telling the kids I would see them in a few hours, I headed up to the Sinclair's to say hi to Becca. The other children were busy working on cleaning up the house as we left, and Liberty was enjoying a few fun moments at the piano. Charles encouraged her to keep up the good work as he left the house and headed up to the Sinclair's home, where Ben, Becca, and I were talking. We discussed the rising tensions in the region as we had done in the past. Our hearts were so heavy to see the country we loved being torn apart by the conflict.

When we got in the car that day to head out of the village, I asked Charles to pray that the Lord would protect and watch over us throughout the day. I do not remember his exact words, but I will always remember him praying. We had prayed together thousands of times in the previous fourteen years, but this prayer, the last he would ever utter, was for our protection as we went to town, for the salvation of souls, and for peace to return in Cameroon. The road out of Bambili was rough and bumpy, making it impossible to move with any real speed. Charles was asking Ben lots of questions as we drove, and I was impressed to begin praying Psalm 91 quietly in the back seat, where I sat next to Lil Charles.

There had been fighting that morning between the Ambas and military forces, so things along the roadside were quiet with fewer people than normal milling about. As we passed several police stations, though, looking for approval to move on, we were given the all clear signal and were relieved to see the police looking rather relaxed. I remember seeing a man walking along the side of the road just seconds before life stood still. At that moment I was thinking all was okay.

We had just come through a roundabout in the village of Bambui, which is right next to Bambili, when I heard a gunshot and glass shattering. In those few seconds, all I remember doing was reaching over, shoving Charles Jr. down, and covering him as a second shot hit our vehicle and more glass shattered.

"Dad, are you OK?" These were the first words uttered, as I heard Ben revving the engine to escape the unknown assailant. Right before Charles Jr. uttered those four words, I was thinking, "Thank God! No one is hit!"

The thought of Charles being hit never even crossed my mind. Somehow, I realized much later, in my subconscious, I had almost viewed him as invincible and indestructible. The next three words I heard my eleven-year-old son scream will haunt me the rest of my life: "Mom, Dad's shot!"

I looked up, still in shock, to see my husband in the seat right in front of me, his head laid over on his shoulder with blood flowing from bullet holes on his head and neck. He was sitting there, still holding the special Garmin GPS he had started using to mark places as we learned our way around the city. It was like he had been hit so quickly, his body just sat there, so straight and upright but unresponsive. I wrapped my arms around him, and I cried out to God like I had never done before in my life. I was soon drenched in my precious husband's blood as I screamed and begged the man I loved to live. I told him he had eight children that needed their daddy and a wife who could not live without him. I told him how sorry I was for failing him so many times. I told him how much I loved him and begged him not to die. I heard him gasping for air as his heart kept beating and he drowned in his own blood. Psalm 23 and Psalm 121 were two passages that came to mind in those minutes we were pleading with God for mercy. My precious son clung to me, screaming and weeping, begging God to save his daddy.

Moments after the shots were fired, we came to the top of a hill where there was a petrol station. We stopped because we saw a group of Cameroonian soldiers standing there. Ben shouted to them that we had a man in the car who had just been shot and begged them for help. They just stood there, as if in shock, as we screamed and begged for help. Finally, they told two doctors who were standing nearby to get in the car and go with us to the closest medical clinic. Part of me wonders why those doctors were with us in that car for the rest of that excruciating trip into Bamenda. They sat there during the drive, listening to the cries that poured from our hearts. Though I do not think I will ever meet either of them again, I pray that they saw Jesus with us in that car because, looking back, I do not have any doubt that He was with us that day, just as He was with His three faithful servants in the fiery furnace of long ago. As someone has written: "God is always on your side, even when things don't make sense. He's for you when the road turns unexpectedly and He's ahead of you when you're not sure how you're going to get through. You will—because He is the strength, the hope, and the One who will never fail you."

During that hour of shock and despair, moments came when I really wondered in my mind if there was a God in heaven who ruled in the affairs of men. How could the God who had given us a complete peace and confidence that He had called us to Cameroon in 2015, brought us through so many victories and trials over those three years of preparation, and answered innumerable prayers, now allow this man, who was completely and utterly sold out to serving his Lord and Savior, be murdered? How could He seemingly lead and guide us through His Word, answer so many prayers for provision, give so many desires of the heart, and now allow every single part of our lives to fall apart? How in the world could any good come from this?

I remember looking at Ben Sinclair as he drove as fast as he could over the bumps and potholes to the nearest clinic. There was blood spattered on him and agony in his face. I can never forget it. I know he was crying out to God in those moments too. God was all we had. Every rough spot we hit would leave Charles' body flopping as I tried to steady his head, neck, and torso and tried to plug as many holes as I could with my fingers. I remember saying, "This has got to be a nightmare!"

Lil Charles wept as he replied, "No, it's worse than a nightmare."

And it was. Every part of me wanted to rewind. *Rewind*. That word holds so much pain and frustration. To where and when would I rewind? When would I restart living life with the one, I had loved with all my heart for so many years? Where would be the first place I would pick to realize that Charles Wesco was my dream come true and the man with whom I wanted to spend the rest of my life? The way I had written my story I was never supposed to have to face any future day of life without him.

After crying and praying our way through traffic in the busy third-world African city of Bamenda, we finally pulled in at the medical clinic, and they opened the gate for us. We could see the look of horror on the Cameroonians' faces as the doctors quickly directed men to carry Charles inside. His head flopped around as they took him out of the vehicle as gently as possible. His once strong body was now like a limp rag. As they pulled his legs out, one of his shoes fell off and was left behind in the car. That would be the last article of clothing I would have to keep as a remembrance from that day. As Charles Jr. and I exited the back seat, I could not understand why the medical personnel were so insistent on taking me in the back, but I am so grateful now that they were. The fact that I was soaked with my husband's blood had not really crossed my mind until they tried to get me to lie down on the cot across from Charles. They kept saying, "Where are you shot?"

Then I realized that the nurses and doctors thought that I was wounded too. I told them that I was not injured and begged them to help my husband. After checking me over a couple times, they finally believed me. Someone came over to help me wash up a little bit. As I stood there, in a clinic that did not even have electricity or running water, facing a mud block wall because they didn't want me looking at my husband, bowlfuls of water were poured over my arms and hands because they were literally coated in thick layers of blood. I remember thinking, "God, we have no one here but You to help us."

Charles' heart kept beating as he lay on that crude bed, and I could hear that he was drowning on his own body fluids. Nurses were yelling, doctors scurrying, and orderlies running around. When I pushed my way to the foot of his bed and saw his face for what would be the last time on earth, I knew beyond a shadow of a doubt that my husband was not going to survive. Though it sounds so strange, those few moments were a precious gift from God to me. He prepared me for the news I would receive later by allowing me to be taken back with Charles, where I never would have been allowed to go if I had not looked like I had been shot. His entire head was distorted, misshaped; blood was coming from his mouth and everywhere else. I could see he had been hit more places than I realized. I worked my way up to his side for a few brief seconds to grab his phone and then was pulled away by the nurses. As they led me from that awful scene, I stopped and rubbed Charles' feet. They were already the color of death and cold, but I rubbed them anyway, wanting to feel him jerk, smile, and give me "the look" he had given me the past fourteen years when I would be ornery and dare to tickle his feet. But this time there was no response, and it was in those moments that I had to surrender my precious husband to the Lord and change my mindset before going back to Charles Jr. and Ben. As I stood there holding the feet of the man, I had loved with all my heart, a verse I had read many times came to mind, "How beautiful are the feet of them that preach the gospel of peace" (Romans 10:15).

So many thoughts were swirling through my head as I was led to the next room, where Charles Jr. sat sobbing. Two Cameroonians were doing their best to comfort him. I knew I could not tell him that his daddy was not going to live, but I also knew I could not pray for Charles to live. At best, I knew he would be a vegetable, and to me, that would have been worse than death because at death my husband would begin his eternal life with the Savior, he loved with all his heart. As I sat down and Charles Jr. sat in my lap weeping and asking me how Daddy was, I told him that Daddy was not doing very well, but the doctors were doing all they could for him. I also told him that we had to pray that God would do what was best for Daddy. Ben was on the phone, looking white as a sheet. I was worried about him too. I knew he had not been shot, but he was in shock and was still thinking Charles was going to make it. He asked me what Charles blood type was, as well as mine, and we found we could both be donors to provide blood for transfusions. We were both more than willing.

People brought us dark chocolate and forced us to chew it up. They made us drink some pop and water. That would be all the food we would eat that day. The doctors did their best to stabilize Charles and then, thanks to an international medical organization that was working there in Bamenda, they were able to transport him via ambulance to a larger Bamenda hospital that was much better equipped.

One of the Cameroonians offered to take us in his car to the hospital, and the three of us got in the back seat, continuing to pray and cry out to the Lord. When we pulled up to the hospital and got out of the car, no one needed to tell us where to go. There was a steady trail of blood all the way to the room where they had taken Charles. We were told we could not see him because a team of doctors was working on him. We were led to a bench outside the building, and we sat down to wait. We again poured our hearts out to the Lord, begging Him to have mercy on Charles. The Lord had already brought me to the place of surrender, but I kept finding myself begging for some incredible miracle. I also remember looking around, thinking the shooter was going to reappear and finish what he had started.

Those minutes seemed like hours, but at last someone came to take us back to talk to the doctors. The scenes play back in my mind almost daily, like a nightmare I can never wake up from. That sterile, white-tiled room smelled strongly of chlorine. When I asked the nurse if she knew anything, she lowered her head. As I look back on those moments, those seconds, those minutes, as the fate of our entire lives, as we had known them, hung in the balance, I cannot explain how the presence of God was so real to us. My heart was breaking, and I wanted more than anything to wake up from the worst possible nightmare, but God was with us in that room in such a real and powerful way. The two doctors came through the doors. I do not remember who spoke first, but I think I asked how my husband was doing. I hoped. The doctors, with bowed heads, began to tell me what exactly had happened to Charles. They explained where he had been hit and what the shots that hit him in the head had done to his brain. As they talked, I realized that all these details could only lead to one outcome. I remember hearing myself, almost as if I were another person talking, ask the doctor, "Is my husband with Jesus?" To which he replied, "Yes, he is."

The following moments are in many ways a blur, but I remember holding onto Charles Jr. and looking at Ben and seeing the agony I was feeling mirrored in his eyes. Part of me felt like all the oxygen in my body had been removed in a moment's time, and I had to tell myself to breathe. The doctors might as well have told me that I, too, had died because it would be months before I would realize that it was all right for me to go on living. The three of us stood there, hugging, praying, and crying together as we tried to process what we had just heard.

Ben told me something in those moments of crying together that will always be treasured words to me. He said that God had made our families coworkers, and though he didn't know what the future looked like for his family or ours, we would always be coworkers. Those words brought so much comfort to my heart as literally everything was crashing around me.

We were taken to another room where we could sit down together and were introduced to the Cameroonian military commander. He asked many questions, looked at Charles' passport, filled in paperwork, and offered condolences to the best of his ability. I remember him asking me if he was correct that we had only been in the country twelve days. In the course of the questioning, I kept falling apart in tears, and my precious son, whose life God had spared, kept encouraging me to stop crying because he feared I was going to get sick. Sometime while we were sitting in that room, the doctors asked me if I wanted to see Charles after they had cleaned up his body as much as possible. As I think back, I wish with all my heart I had said yes, but at the time, I could not stand the thought of gazing into his lifeless, mangled face and holding a cold hand that would never squeeze mine again. I also was very concerned that Charles Jr. feel as secure as possible, and I didn't want to add any extra trauma to his heart by leaving him for any amount of time. I remember telling the doctor, "That is just his body. He is not there. My husband is in heaven with Jesus."

As I think about the events that occurred in that room, I realize there were special gifts from God in that darkest of times. A Christian Cameroonian doctor, who had been at the first clinic, stayed with Charles the whole time until after he was pronounced dead. This man was used by God to say words to Charles Jr. and to me that will forever stick in our memories. He put his arm around Charles Jr. and with love and compassion in his voice told him that God had a very special purpose for his life and encouraged him to stay faithful to the God of his father. He knelt beside me and said, "Thank you for coming to my country. Thank you that your husband was willing to shed his blood for my people. Your husband's death is not in vain. I believe his death is the spark that God will use to bring the beginning of revival in Cameroon." Those words were gifts from God!

As we sat there, a white lady entered the room, sat down beside me, and held my hand. Though she spoke some English, I remember very little of what she said to me, but her presence and compassion meant the world just then. I soon learned that she was part of a special medical organization, and she offered to take Charles Jr. and me back to their headquarters to rest. The other option was to stay there in the hospital and rest on some cots. Part of me was terrified to leave that room, to face the outside, and to get in a vehicle again. I also didn't want to leave Ben to deal with everything by himself, but he thought we should go with Esperanza, so we did. (*Esperanza* means "hope.") Whenever I think of the people God brought into our lives that day, I marvel at how that sweet lady, whom I had never met before but will never forget as long as I live, conveyed so much hope and love in her words and actions, ministering to us in countless ways throughout the rest of that day. Esperanza and the others there were gifts from God!

As we walked back through the hospital and out the entrance to get in the vehicle, the trail of my husband's blood was now mingled with our trail of tears. After a short drive to the organization's headquarters, we were led up two flights of stairs and into a quaint and comfortable little apartment. The ladies who lived there quickly made their bed for us. Esperanza gave me clothes to change into, offering to take mine to clean for me. They gave Charles Jr. a clean shirt as well. As I stood at the bathroom sink and looked in the mirror for the first time that day, I saw a sight that left me sobbing. I saw a woman in the mirror, covered from head to foot in blood, who had a look in her eyes that terrified me—a look of shock, fear disbelief, and deadness. But as I stood there staring at that face, I once again found myself at the throne of my Savior, telling Him He was all I could cling to.

Charles Jr. lay down and soon appeared to be asleep. I lay down, craving sleep, craving unconsciousness. But when I closed my eyes, all I could see was the day's events replaying. My brain was on high alert, and every sound from the streets below turned into gunshots in my brain. It was torture. Why had Charles died? Why had God taken him and not me? How in the world was I going to live without him?

When could we get back to Bambili and our families? How was I going to tell the children their daddy was gone? Did we have to leave the place that had just become home? How was I supposed to pack up the house we had just finished setting up? What was Ben doing? Where was Charles' body? What were they doing with him at the hospital?

Continual questions became a strong current, which continued to take me over the side of a waterfall in my mind.

Since I couldn't sleep, I decided to go back out into the main living area, and soon Charles Jr. joined me. There was a young man, who was sitting there working quietly. He was also keeping a watchful eye on us, asking how we were doing and if we needed anything. Because of his profession, he had been trained to help in trauma situations and knew the right questions. He didn't pretend to know or understand everything we were feeling, but he listened, encouraged, and sought to give us comfort. He understood that I was terrified to go outside the apartment or have Charles Jr. or me near a window. He offered water, knowing both of us were severely dehydrated. He was another angel that God had lined up ahead of time to help us that day.

As we had done so many times in the last few hours, Charles Jr. and I started praying together. Prayer was the only thing that was going to hold together anything of our lives and sanity that was not already completely shattered. I prayed for Uncle Ben, for all of our family back in Bambili, and then I prayed, through tears, for the person who had killed Charles. I don't remember all my words, but my heart's cry was forgiveness and begging God for that person's salvation. My husband was in heaven, but I knew that whoever shot Charles was headed to a Christless eternity, and that broke my heart. As we finished praying, our new friend looked at me with a very odd expression on his face and said, "Can I ask you a question?"

I nodded, and he said, "I am very confused. I have never seen someone respond to a traumatic event the way you are! You should be filled with anger right now—that is one of the first steps of grieving. But instead, you are praying with your son. You just prayed with forgiveness for the man who murdered your husband! I have never seen something so . . . so noble! How can you do that?"

Thus, began ministry after Charles' death. I never would have planned or expected to be giving the gospel to someone under those circumstances, but it was a divine opportunity. I don't remember exactly how I replied, but I shared Jesus and His love with him.

The remaining hours of that day are a blur, but at some point, Ben came from the hospital to join us. He told me about Cameroonian brothers in Christ coming to lovingly carry Charles' body for him, about the doctor who was so moved by Charles' death, about the fact that we were stuck in Bamenda for the time being. Hopefully it would be safe to return to Bambili on Wednesday. My father called from the States. He was doing his best to work out funeral arrangements there. The funeral home had been called, there was a list of paperwork they needed, and family members were working on details to get us out of the country. He told me they needed an obituary written. I then found out that the story of Charles' death had circulated far and wide, which sent me into another form of shock. The US ambassador called, offering his condolences and asking how they could assist us. I remember putting my head in my hands more times than I could count, just wanting to curl up and die. There was so much I had to do, so much that had to be thought through, and my brain felt like complete mush. "Lord, help me," became the moment by moment cry of my heart.

I had cried so much that there were no more tears left. As Ben and I sat together late that night, both still in shock over the day's events, talking through numerous things, he pulled Charles' wallet out of his pocket, along with copied pages from Charles' Bible. Charles had started memorizing the book of Hebrews and was working on chapter 2. I guess he was hoping for time to review it that day and had those pages in his pocket. Ben handed them to me. Then he pulled out his key ring, and as he did, my heart broke because on that key ring hung a gold ring. The ring had "I love you 11-20-04" engraved on the inside. It was the ring that I had placed on the finger of the man with whom I planned to spend the rest of my life. Now that ring was being handed back to me, and my heart broke all over again. I quickly discovered there were more tears—an endless supply. We worked on writing Charles' obituary late into the night and then finally prayed for peace and rest, both of us knowing there would be no sleep that night. Ben went to his room in another part of the building. I took a sleeping pill the doctor had given me and lay down on the bed beside my son. It was not a night of sleep, but thanks to the sleeping pill, at least I could close my eyes and not relive everything the whole night.

The later hours of that fateful day found me thinking about my heroes Jim and Elisabeth Elliot, remembering how I had often wondered how she could love and not hate those who had killed her husband. How could there be a love that strong? Now I found myself in a similar situation, and there was no anger and no hatred but a love and compassion for the killer! I cried, thinking of the fate he faced without a Savior from sin. I marveled at the fact that I cared so deeply for his soul. I knew that was not coming from me, but from Jesus, who lived in me and who loved and had died for the person who shot my husband. Yes, there was a love that strong. It was that love that had drawn us to Cameroon. It was that love that gave us joy through the long years of deputation. It was that love, that had given us joy, peace, and contentment in a foreign land. Even in the middle of so much grief and shock, that same love now flooded my heart in a way I would have never imagined possible before that day—love for the killer and for the country I had been committed to ministering in for the rest of my life. And because of that love, my heart broke, realizing our time as missionaries, living in Cameroon, was fast coming to an end.

Wednesday morning found me opening my eyes, staring at the ceiling, and wondering where I was and how I had gotten there. Reality sank in quickly. My mind raced, replaying everything that had transpired in the previous twenty-four hours. I found myself wanting to completely give up on life. My husband was not there beside me as he had been for almost fourteen years. Instead, his namesake, who had seen his father get shot, lay there sleeping. That first morning after losing Charles, I prayed, "Lord, I can't get through today without You. I don't know how to tell my children that their daddy is gone. I don't know how to even live life going forward. You promise Your mercies are new every morning, and I need Your mercies for today!"

It was barely light outside when I got up and ventured out into the living area. I looked outside and finally got up the courage to go close to the doorway of the balcony and look out over the city of Bamenda. Tears came to my eyes as I thought about how often Charles and I had talked about this city, how we longed to see it reached with the gospel, how we dreamed of starting different outreaches to minister to the multitudes of people there. I cried because I was going to have to leave, not knowing if or when I would ever be able to come back to this place that had held part of my heart for over two years.

The sunrise brought so many emotions. I dreaded having to live. Twenty-four hours before, I had felt like a fairly pulled-together, happy missionary wife and mother; now I was a broken missionary widow with eight children in a foreign country. Charles Jr. was up by 6:30, struggling with all of the reality hitting him. I called Ben, and he came down to the apartment. We sat together and prayed for a while before heading to the kitchen area. We all forced ourselves to eat a little something, knowing that this day was going to be, in some ways, as traumatic as the previous one had been.

Not long after breakfast, Ben left to return to the hospital. So much paperwork had to be taken care of before we could return to Bambili, and there was precious little time. Pain started coming in waves that morning, as my heart and chest literally felt like they were broken. Breathing hurt! I was so thankful that the pharmacist had provided medicine to help keep it under control. My new friend handed me a printed sheet of paper that morning, kindly telling me that I was going to need help that he couldn't provide. He hoped that the few bullet points he had typed up for me would help me just a little bit. I only read the list once, and the paper was lost later in the chaos of the day, but there were concepts on that paper that I didn't realize would be a part of my life going forward. Post-traumatic stress disorder (PTSD), flashbacks, panic attacks, pain, hyperventilating—these were terms that didn't mean much to me that day as my brain fought to even think, but I'll never forget that young man's kindness. He was so concerned for my well-being because he knew better than I did what I was facing.

Ben returned and told me that we had to meet with the police to file a report about the shooting. Leaving the place that had become my "safe place," I held on to my son's hand. As we followed Ben, we walked right past the car with its shattered windows. So many horrifying memories! But I had to focus on staying sane for my son there beside me. We sat down with the police officer in a shop across the street and recounted the previous day's events. As I sat there in a daze, Ben and the officer went out to take a closer look at Ben's car. When they returned, Ben and I compared notes and confirmed that the shots had all come from the right side of the vehicle. Ben also informed me that none of us should have walked away from the vehicle. We all should have been either severely wounded or dead. There were bullet holes in every seat. There was no explanation for the fact that the three of us had survived untouched, other than the mighty hand of God. The angel of the Lord truly had encamped around us and protected us!

Looking out the window of that shop while waiting for Ben, I saw angels standing around and sitting with my son. They were not dressed in white and did not have wings or halos. They were Cameroonian brothers in Christ—men Charles had kept in constant contact with throughout our years on deputation; men who were there at the hospital to carry the body of Charles to the morgue; men who were willing to be there with us when we felt so alone, providing Mambo bars (Cameroonian version of chocolate), drinks, and comfort that I cannot even put into words. Those brothers in Christ became as dear to me that day as any person on earth! They stood there like a wall around my son; they sat beside him, with their arms around him, offering the love of Christ in an incredibly tangible way. Jesus shone through them! They asked me over and over again if there was anything they could do for me. They were angels sent from God to us that day.

Our next stop was the government office in Bamenda, where we would get Charles' death certificate. "Ashya" (the Cameroonian term for "I'm sorry") filled my ears over and over again as people in that office sought to convey their sympathy. One of the sweetest memories in my mind from that day is of sitting in the government office, waiting for my turn to get help with the death certificate. Through the window I saw a truck full of Cameroonian soldiers in full gear, looking like they were ready for battle. One of the Cameroonian brothers in Christ ministering to us went over to the truck and began handing a gospel tract to each of the soldiers. I smiled, as they sat there, opened up the tracts, and began reading them. To think of how many were getting the opportunity to hear the gospel gave me the only joy I could hold on to that day.

Miraculously, Charles' death certificate was filled out, stamped, and ready to go in a very short amount of time. With that in hand, I went with Ben to another office to be interviewed again, this time by the Cameroonian military commanders of the Northwest Region. Recounting the story once more was torture, but the Lord got us through it. When we were done, we went outside and prepared to begin our journey back to Bambili. By this time, it had become clear that we would have to evacuate the English region that day, and our time was running short. My brain swirled, as I wondered what I was going to say to my kids, how I was going to face them, what I was going to grab, how I was going to leave behind everything that had been our dream for over three years. The car ride was silent as Ben and I sat on either side of Charles Jr., our minds all racing. As we neared the place where Charles was shot, terror flooded my heart, and I just wanted to wake up from the nightmare. All over again, I heard the gunshots, glass shattering, and Charles Jr. screaming, "Dad's hit!"

We rolled up our windows, pled with God for safety, and Brother Paul drove as fast as he dared. There are no words to describe all the emotions that flooded that little car. I think in our hearts all of us were before the throne of grace, pleading for help in that desperate time of need. For me, there was a very real sense of dread in the air as we neared the village, and my heart cried out to the Lord in agony, wondering why I had to do what was coming. Ben asked me if I wanted him to tell the kids what had happened, and I was so grateful for his willingness to do that heartbreaking task.

"Lord, couldn't there have been another way for you to accomplish Your goals, to glorify Yourself? Yet not my will, but Thine be done."

10

"WHERE'S DADDY?"

We passed the kids walking back down the road to our house as we pulled up near the Sinclair's home. Becca and I hugged and cried. Liberty and I hugged and cried. As we walked toward the house, a couple of the of the children ran up to me, asking, "Mommy, where's Daddy?"

Daniel asked, "Mom, where's Dad? Did he get arrested or something?"

Oh, if only!

As we walked in the house, I took note that all the suitcases we had brought were lined up neatly in the front hallway, along with the children's backpacks. We gathered everyone in the parlor, and all sat together on the floor. Brother Barnabus, who, less than thirty-six hours before, had sat eating breakfast with us, now sat in the corner of the room weeping. There was a solemn hush over the room when Ben opened his Bible and quietly read Psalm 23. He then gave the children a brief synopsis of the past day's events. The sights and sounds of my precious children's hearts breaking will forever haunt me. Weeping and sobbing filled the room, as the reality that their Daddy was gone pierced each precious heart. In those moments, the Lord brought to my mind a cherished verse, which I cried out in those minutes of overwhelming grief: "The Lord is my rock, and my fortress, and my deliverer; my God, my strength, in whom I will trust; my buckler, and the horn of my salvation, and my high tower" (Psalm 18:2).

There was nothing else to say that mattered as we sat weeping and clinging to each other. I wished in those moments that I had had eight arms, one for each of my children. I wish time had stood still as the children dealt with the shock and horrific news of their daddy's death. I wish we could have all just sat there together the rest of the day, holding and comforting one another. But time was against us; the minutes were quickly ticking by. When I looked up from comforting one of my children, my eyes met Becca's and I saw the worried expression on her face. She looked at her watch, and I knew we had to get moving.

"Kids, we have to stop crying now. We have only a little while to gather up your most important, favorite things, put them in your backpacks, and then we have to leave."

I felt like the worst mother who had ever walked the earth. In less than thirty minutes, my children found out their father was killed and then were told to stop crying because we had to focus on preparing to evacuate as quickly as possible.

"We have to leave? We just got here; this is our home! What do we take? We are going to have to leave almost everything behind? Why do we have to leave?" Questions poured from the lips of my children as they looked at me in disbelief through their tears. Part of me really wanted to scream and cry out in anguish in those moments. My own broken heart was weeping over those same questions and was being ground into powder. But God's overwhelming grace and strength became so real as I tried to explain to the children that they needed to trust Mommy, Uncle Ben, and Aunt Becca and just obey.

Only God could have given the focus and strength that was needed in those following minutes as we grabbed and threw things into a few suitcases and footlockers. Liberty and one of the Sinclair's daughters had already worked hard before we got back to pack up many of the necessities.

I will never cease to be amazed at the clarity of thought God gave them in the midst of shock and grief to pack so many things that were vital. She had already gotten all the paperwork as well as our matching Cameroonian outfits, knowing I would want them for the funeral. A few outfits for each child were packed as well as things around the house that she knew were special to me. The day before Charles was killed, I had completely organized his closet, putting all the important papers together in a storage cube. Although his office was not set up yet, he had put all the important hard drives and such things together in the drawer of his desk. Because things were freshly organized, it made evacuation packing much easier. Daniel and Charles made a careful search for all the electronics, cords, charging devices, and such that we needed to take. Since Liberty had not packed any clothes for me, I went into the master bedroom not knowing what I wanted to grab. As I entered the room, new waves of emotion hit me. As I looked at our mattress on the floor, my eyes caught sight of Charles' pillow. Oh, how I wanted to lie down, bury my head in that pillow, and let out all the anguish that filled my heart. But there was no time. I picked up his pillow and hugged it for a few moments, weeping, and wishing so much I could kiss the face of the man who had rested his head on it less than forty-eight hours before. Then I laid it down and turned to the closet, trying to focus on our evacuation. I grabbed Charles' dress shoes, his robe, his glasses, my Bible and toiletry necessities, and some clothes. As I worked, literally throwing things in the footlocker, feeling like I was having a nightmare. I was in a hurry but unable to move fast enough. Brother Angel came up beside me and patiently but urgently said, "Sister, we have to go!"

I knew our time was up. It was time to leave the place that had been home in my heart for over two years. We were leaving the house looking as it might have if the rapture had occurred—food sitting out; laundry lying on the couch; grain, oil, and other bread-making supplies on the counter where Charles had left them the morning before. As I quickly walked through the house one last time, my eyes caught sight of the decal verses Liberty and I had worked so hard to press onto those rough cement-block walls. We had put Isaiah 40:31, one of Charles' favorite verses, on the big wall in the dining room; Zephaniah 3:17 and Philippians 4:13 boldly stood out on the walls of the large hall that ran down the center of the house. As I took one last look at those verses, I was reminded that our Savior, who had led us to that place, was still walking beside us, and He was not going to leave or forsake us.

I walked out of the house and up the path towards the church van, where the children were already gathered. Men, women, and children stood along the edge of the road with looks of sympathy, sorrow, and shock on their faces. I hugged several of the ladies and shook hands with the men, saying goodbye to them through my tears. Disbelief still filled my heart at the fact that I would never again this side of heaven see these people that I had just met and yet loved so much. We drove the short distance up the road to the Sinclair's house, where they began loading their carry-ons and backpacks. My heart broke for them, realizing that they were leaving behind fifteen years of their life, not knowing if they would ever see their home again. Many tearful goodbyes were shared between all the children and adults, and we lifted our hearts together in prayer before the Lord one last time there in Bambili, as American and Cameroonian brothers and sisters in Christ, bonded together by love, friendship, and suffering. It mattered not that we were from two different continents, countries, cultures, and colors. We all knew in those precious moments that what really mattered was that we belonged to and were loved and cared for by the same heavenly Father, who in His sovereign plan had chosen to take one of us to Himself but in His mercy had spared the rest of us to carry on His plan for the rest of our lives.

That poor little church van suffered its own trauma that afternoon as we all piled into it, children sitting on top of adults with some even squished between legs on the floor. "Sardines in a can" is not even ample to describe how tight we were in that vehicle! Brother Angel will always hold such a special place in my heart because of the grace and peace of God that showed through him that day. As we drove down that hill away from the Sinclair's house and headed out of the village, I felt a strong sense of evil and danger surrounding us. When I tried to pray, the only words that would come out of my heart were "Lord, blind their eyes!"

If there was anyone lurking there, ready to do us harm, God indeed heard and answered our prayers. Just as God parted the Red Sea for His people to pass through safely, He put His divine hedge of safely around that overloaded van and protected us. As we neared the spot where Charles had been shot, I knew I was not the only one who was inwardly recoiling. There was no strength or courage in me to pass over that road again. I will never forget hearing what sounded like the voice of an angel begin singing as Angel began lifting his heart and voice before the Lord in worship and praise. Soon that crammed little church van, filled with trauma, shock, and grief, became a place of worship and adoration to our Savior. As we passed by the place where Charles had received his summons to Glory, we lifted our voices, singing together through our tears:

He Leadeth Me

He leadeth me, O blessed thought!
O words with heav'nly comfort fraught!
Whate'er I do, where'er I be
Still 'tis God's hand that leadeth me.

Chorus:
He leadeth me, He leadeth me, by His own hand He leadeth me;
His faithful foll'wer I would be, for by His hand He leadeth me.

Sometimes 'mid scenes of deepest gloom,
Sometimes where Eden's bowers bloom,
By waters still, o'er troubled sea,
Still 'tis His hand that leadeth me.

To Die Is Gain

Chorus

Lord, I would place my hand in Thine,
Nor ever murmur nor repine;
Content, whatever lot I see,
Since 'tis my God that leadeth me.

Chorus

And when my task on earth is done,
When by Thy grace the vict'ry's won,
E'en death's cold wave I will not flee,
Since God through Jordan leadeth me.

—Joseph H. Gilmore, Public Domain

On our way through Bamenda to meet up with a military escort, we stopped at the bakery, where Ben got some bread, so that the children would have something to eat. Then we continued on our way to the place where we were supposed to meet up with the escort. Around this time Ben received a call from a friend saying that a gun battle had broken out in Bambili shortly after we got out of the village.

We watched in amazement, as the BIRs (Cameroon's version of special forces) appeared, with their armored vehicles, as well as a truck full of soldiers with their weapons at the ready. At first, they insisted that we all get into their armored vehicles for safety's sake, but Ben kindly explained that everyone really wanted to just stay together in our van. Finally, the commander conceded but, on the condition, that if they ordered us to do it later, we would obey. Ben agreed. Within a few moments, soldiers began bringing us bottled water and pop. It was such an incredible blessing to all of us since drinking had not been a priority that day. We dispersed it throughout the crowded vehicle, along with more bread, and went on our way. Military vehicles went in front of us and behind. I had to marvel at the goodness of God. One of my biggest fears about our evacuation had been the fact that we would be prime targets throughout the first part of the journey. God heard my cries for protection and answered through those soldiers.

The trip was uneventful for the most part, with only one bathroom stop for the children. A sweet moment I'll always remember took place at the petrol station where we stopped. Military personnel surrounded our vehicle like bodyguards as we got out. Emmy clung to my skirt, looking around apprehensively. One of the soldiers pulled a Mambo bar out of his shirt, broke off a piece, bent down, and offered it to her. Emmy's love of chocolate took over, and she tried to take the whole bar out of his hand. It made for some smiles, but we told Emmy she could only have the piece, which she gladly took!

At one point, shortly after we had crossed into the French side, the gearshift acted up on the van. We had to wait awhile until the men figured out was wrong and got it working. We arrived in Bafoussam late that evening, with the military escorting us all the way to the house of the missionary friends with whom we were to spend the night.

Those missionaries were such a blessing to us that evening. They fed us delicious soup, which was a great comfort food, and then gave up many of their beds, so we would all have places to sleep. We had some sweet time to sit and unwind for the first time in over twenty-four hours. Though we were still in a daze, being able to sit down, feel safe, and breathe a little easier was such a blessing.

As the adults were sitting together, Joseph came over to me and said, "Mom, Charles said he knows what Dad has probably been doing ever since he got to heaven! He has had all the apostles lined up and is asking them all his long list of questions about things from the Bible! Paul is probably like, 'Charles, I've been sitting here talking with you for twelve hours now! Are we almost done?'"

We all started laughing—the first time we had laughed together since Monday evening. I looked at Joseph with tears in my eyes and said, "You boys need to always remember all those special times you got to have with Daddy while we were on deputation. All the times he would spend telling you about different things from the Bible, all the things he did to make the trips special and . . ."

Joseph got a wistful, thoughtful look on his face. Then with a mischievous smile, he said, "Yes, and all the spankings!"

At that, there was hearty laughter around the table, and we all had a few moments of reprieve from the waves of sorrow and grief. I will always be thankful for the wonderful sense of humor God placed in my thirdborn son. The close, loving, and trusting relationship he had had with his dad still gave him stability, even after his death. That night Joseph's ability to bring joy to a room was an extra special gift from the Lord.

We all prayed together and then dispersed to our different assigned places to sleep. Even though I was so tired, sleep came and went throughout the night, as I dealt with my own upheaval, along with Emmy's. She would cry out for Daddy, asking where he was. I would get her back to sleep and then lie there and cry. At one point, I got up to walk around, but that woke Emmy up, resulting in more cuddle time with her. Sleep brought nightmares. How I wished for daylight and morning to come. It finally did, and then began the scramble of figuring out what needed to happen next. People were taking turns in the shower and eating breakfast. The men worked on securing a bus and driver to take us from Bafoussam to Yaoundé. Mrs. B made popcorn for us to take on the road later that day and offered to help us start repacking our luggage to prepare for the flight back to the States. Her help was a tremendous blessing because my brain was completely fogged by that point.

In the middle of packing, some of our missionary friends, who had also had to evacuate via the missionary plane, came to see us. It was our first time to see them since Charles' death, and many tears were shed. Our lives had been completely and utterly turned upside down, and we all were in a state of shock. It was such a blessing and gift from the Lord to spend some time together before we headed south toward Yaoundé.

Sometime in the afternoon, after prayer together and saying goodbye, we all climbed in the bus that would take us to Yaoundé. It was not a comfortable vehicle by any stretch of the imagination, but at that point comfort was not a concern. As we traveled along, I realized that sounds were my worst enemy. Every time we hit a pothole, my heart would race, and I had to work to keep myself from freaking out. The sharp sounds translated into gunshots in my tired and traumatized brain, resulting in flashbacks and many tears during those hours of travel. I worried about Ben and Charles Jr., who were sitting in the very front. My brain would play horrible tricks on me, and I would visualize the two of them getting shot just like Charles had been. Many prayers and cries for the Lord's help and strength rose from my heart during that long trip.

One of the special memories from that day of traveling was buying Cameroonian fast food. There were no McDonald's, Burger Kings, or Arby's, but there were people selling roasted field corn and dried plantains along the road. It's amazing how good food of any kind tastes when you're really hungry, and plantains are pretty good! It was a fun learning experience for us, and we really enjoyed getting to feel that part of the culture before leaving the country.

Yaoundé finally came into view late Thursday evening, and we marveled at how different the atmosphere was there compared to the ghost town/curfew atmosphere of the Northwest Region at night. How our hearts rejoiced when we finally arrived at the mission housing, where we would stay till our flights back to the States late Saturday night.

Those couple of days in Yaoundé were much needed. Both families needed some time alone together to process life and all the changes that had occurred so quickly. We settled in as best we could Thursday evening, knowing that Friday would be a big day since the ambassador was coming. Friday morning everyone got cleaned up, dressed as nicely as possible under the circumstances, and prepared for the visit with Ambassador Peter Barlerin and his wife. I had talked to the children ahead of time about the importance of showing honor and respect for him. I asked them if they would be willing to sing together for him. When he arrived and introductions had been made, we all sat down together and spent some time visiting. The children sang for him and his wife, and we had a sweet time together. I figured out quickly that he was a very kind, down-to-earth person. Before long, my little children were crowded around him, talking and having a great time.

After his aide and I had finished going over the necessary paperwork regarding Charles' body, we all went outside together and took a picture. Caleb managed to get held by the Ambassador for that memorable event and kept Mommy praying that he would not say anything too embarrassing. All the kids thought it was pretty amazing that the ambassador had a full security detail. Their excitement and awe made everyone smile. We will always be so incredibly grateful for all the help US government officials gave us, especially Ambassador Barlerin and the many embassy aides who helped us till we boarded the plane to head home. God used each of them to bring comfort and peace to our hearts, and we are so thankful for each one who had a part in helping get us home.

In a statement released by his office, Vice President Mike Pence called Charles "a believer, loving father, and pillar of his Indiana community" and went on to say, "Charles lost his life while he and his family were sharing the gospel in Cameroon. . . . Karen and I will be praying for Charles' wife Stephanie, their eight beautiful children, and all those whose lives had been touched by his work and witness. And we will pray that they take comfort in the sure knowledge that Charles heard those words 'Well done good and faithful servant.'" The governor of Indiana, Eric J. Holcomb, also released an official statement regarding Charles' death, which was encouraging to us.

While we were there in Yaoundé, we felt overwhelmed by the outpouring of love we experienced from other missionaries in the surrounding area. They brought in meals for all of us, sacrificing greatly their own time and resources since everything had to be made from scratch and there were so many of us. They lovingly made sure all our needs were met to the best of their ability. Some of them also took up an offering for the children, which was very sacrificial, so that the children could take part of Cameroon home with them—

Cameroonian soccer shirts for the boys and little necklaces for the girls—something they will always treasure.

One of my sweetest memories from those last few days before our departure from Cameroon was when some missionary ladies and Cameroonian sisters in Christ came to see me. We had a prayer time together, and I will never forget the beautiful prayer of one of the Cameroonian women. As she lifted her heart before the Lord in prayer, she asked the Lord to give me "strength for today, and bright hope for tomorrow." I will never forget the sweet and precious gift those words were to me that day. They come from a well-known hymn, which we had sung along the way on our evacuation journey, but somehow hearing her pray them was an extra special gift that day. They were exactly what God knew I needed to hear as a new chapter of life was about to begin for us.

Late Friday evening, my uncle and my sister arrived from the States. They had come to help us make the journey back. Seeing them caused hurt and gave comfort all at the same time. So many painful emotions filled my heart during those days that it felt like it would burst at times.

Saturday was the last day we would spend in Cameroon. My heart broke that morning at the realization that I would soon leave the country where my husband's blood had been shed because of his willingness to spread the love of Christ out of the heart God had given him for the people there. Every part of me wanted to find a way we could stay. Surely, we didn't have to leave. Surely, God wasn't taking us out right after we had arrived. Surely, there could be another way! But there wasn't. Even though a part of my heart had died and been buried in Cameroon the day Charles was killed and even though I wanted to stay, the harsh reality was that I had eight children to think about. They had to be my focus. We worked at packing up our luggage, making luggage tags out of gorilla tape and giving the missionaries in Yaoundé the things that we could leave behind and that would be a blessing to them. We force-fed food so that it would not be wasted. Some of us went into the city to have a little bit of "fun" one last time at the market. We walked around outside so the little ones could run and play before having to be cooped up in an airplane for hours. I remember soaking up all the sights and sounds around me, trying to stamp them on my heart forever.

As evening approached, Ben came and told me that the embassy had called because they needed clothes for Charles to be buried in. I already knew what he would have wanted to wear, so we dug through the luggage till we found a pair of his favorite everyday black pants and the shirt we had made for him in Cameroon on our survey trip in 2015. Though no one would see, I would know that we were all wearing our Cameroonian outfits together one last time at his funeral, and somehow that was special to me.

Around 8:30 p.m. the entourage of vehicles arrived from the embassy to transport us to the airport. Luggage was loaded and then people. The children and I were provided a beautiful fifteen-passenger van to travel in. As we drove out of the compound, I knew there were two ways we could spend the twenty minutes it would take us to reach the airport—in tears or in song. We chose to sing! So many praises filled that vehicle as we made our way through Yaoundé to the airport. We sang of God's goodness, His faithfulness, bowing the knee to our King, our decision to follow Jesus, and so much more. As our driver pulled up along the curb outside the airport, he turned to us and said, "Thank you so much for ministering to me!"

I had praised the Lord in my heart as I realized that because of our decision to focus on Jesus during that ride, God had been glorified and able to work in the heart of our Cameroonian driver.

The next couple of hours were a blur as we went through the complicated processes of being able to get on the plane. We were so thankful for the embassy aides who assisted us along the way and helped expedite getting us where we needed to go at each step. Thankfully, there were no serious complications, and we were on board and ready for takeoff in plenty of time. As our plane headed down the runway, tears fell in abundance. It truly felt at that moment like my heart was being left in Cameroon even though my body was on a plane headed back to America. I felt heartbroken to be leaving

Cameroon and Africa less than three weeks after arrival and without the man I loved.

Hours later, we landed in Paris, where we were given gracious care and attention, including a beautiful place to stay during our layover. But there was a sense of relief, as we prepared to board our Delta Airlines flight, bound for America. We arrived in Indianapolis, Sunday evening, November 4, 2018 (just five days after Charles' death) and were met by multiple family members at the airport.

11

LIVING IN SHOCK

The next few days became a blur, as loss of sleep, jet lag, shock, and preparations for Charles' funeral all happened at once. I found myself writing checks for cemetery grave plots, paying funeral home expenses, and trying to interact with people coming in and out constantly. There were times that week that all I wanted to do was curl up and die. God was so gracious in providing friends who tried to help in every way they could. We were so thankful for the outpouring of love from around the world. The GoFundMe account that had been set up went crazy with responses. Some of our best friends began an Amazon wish list for us, and many people began helping us replace everything we had to leave behind in Cameroon. Because so many people cared for us and loved us, the children had warm clothing provided, shoes, toys, and many other things they needed. Some very dear friends came from Ohio and gave up a couple weeks of their lives to help in a multitude of ways and helped organize luggage, clothing, and a myriad of other details that needed to be taken care of. I'll never forget when my sister told me she was taking me shopping to get clothes and shoes. (All I had was flip flops and clothes for a hot climate, and it was cold and snowing!) When I told her, I didn't have the money for that, she calmly replied that my friend's church had taken up a love offering for me to go get whatever I needed. It overwhelmed and humbled me that people would show such love and generosity to us when I felt that we, in no way, deserved special treatment. Meals were provided each day that week, and friends brought in groceries. The Lord showed us daily that He was faithful and had not forgotten us.

Songs in the night became one of God's greatest gifts to me during that week. Many mornings I would wake up with the words of the chorus or verse of a beautiful hymn already running through my mind before I was fully conscious. During those days the Lord solidified in my thinking the impact of godly music on the heart and mind of someone who is going through grief and trauma.

One of the greatest heroes in my life had always been my dad, but from the day Charles died and in those grueling weeks that followed, my dad proved to be even more amazing than I could have dreamed possible. Even though his heart was breaking too, he poured himself into helping and supporting me through the many different facets of preparation for the funeral and burial services. He, along with our church family, gave and sacrificed greatly to help us during that time.

The day of the private funeral was cold and blustery. Thanks to my sister and a friend, all the children's clothes were prepared ahead of time and ready for them to get dressed. We dressed, ate breakfast, and gathered up everything we needed for the day. As we headed toward the church, even though my heart was completely broken, it was filled with the complete peace of the Lord. When we walked into the foyer, straight ahead of me at the front of the auditorium, I could see Charles' coffin with a beautiful spray of lilies and roses covering the top. After laying out his Bible, his shoe from the day he died, a couple of pictures, and some other special memorials from Cameroon, I walked with the children to the front of the church. As I gazed at the wooden box holding the earthly remains of the man I had loved, I remembered his words to me on our honeymoon fourteen years earlier. "When I die, I just want to be buried in a wooden box—nothing fancy!"

To Die Is Gain

Caleb saying goodbye to his daddy's earthly body

There was nothing fancy about his coffin, but how beautiful it was to me that God even gave him his heart's desire in that detail! It had been made from beautiful wood in Cameroon and had a plate on top inscribed with his name and place of death—Cameroon, the place where he had left his heart.

The funeral was a beautiful testimony to a life well lived for Jesus. Family members gave testimonies and sang songs that spoke of the kind of life Charles had lived—a life wholly committed to his Lord. Pastor Don Barth preached a message that was comforting and challenging to me. Then came the burial service at the cemetery. My heart broke in pieces as I gazed at Charles' coffin, knowing that after I left, it would be put in the ground and covered with dirt. As everyone gathered there sang "Jesus is All the World to Me," my heart cried out to God for strength to sing, to keep going for my Savior and my children.

Jesus Is All The World To Me

*Jesus is all the world to me,
My life, my joy, my all;
He is my strength from day to day,
Without Him I would fall.
When I am sad, to Him I go,
No other one can cheer me so;
When I am sad, He makes me glad,
He's my Friend.*

*Jesus is all the world to me,
My Friend in trials sore;
I go to Him for blessings, and
He gives them o'er and o'er.
He sends the sunshine and the rain,
He sends the harvest's golden grain;
Sunshine and rain, harvest of grain,
He's my Friend.*

*Jesus is all the world to me,
And true to Him I'll be;
Oh, how could I this Friend deny,
When He's so true to me?
Following Him I know I'm right,
He watches o'er me day and night;
Following Him by day and night,
He's my Friend.*

Jesus is all the world to me,

> *I want no better Friend;*
> *I trust Him now, I'll trust Him when*
> *Life's fleeting days shall end.*
> *Beautiful life with such a Friend,*
> *Beautiful life that has no end;*
> *Eternal life, eternal joy,*
> *He's my Friend.*

—Will L. Thompson, Public Domain

The following Monday, November 12, we headed up to South Bend to Community Baptist Church, where the public memorial service for Charles was going to be held. As we pulled in, I was overwhelmed at the number of cars that were in the parking lot. Inside there were people everywhere. Everyone I passed was so sweet and compassionate. I was so thankful for family members who took care of all the children for me during the time before and after the service and protected them from the public eye. Before the service began, I went into the room where the children were, and together we prayed that God would be glorified and that He would use the service to lead people to salvation and surrender. I firmly believe God heard and answered those prayers.

Beautiful music and testimonies were once again shared, this time with the world. Our veteran missionary friend from Cameroon gave the plea for more laborers to go to the white harvest fields, to pick up the mantle that fell from Charles' shoulders as he left for Heaven. As a coworker and friend, Ben Sinclair gave his own tribute to Charles and summarized Charles' life in four simple sentences:

- *"Charles Wesco esteemed others better than himself.*
- *Charles preferred obedience to Christ above his personal safety and health.*
- *Charles loved the people of Cameroon more than he loved his own comfort and ease.*

> • *Charles loved Christ and His glorious gospel more than he loved his own life."*

Then Ben read this statement from me:

> *"All the way my Savior leads me. What have I to ask beside?*
> *Can I doubt His tender mercies, who through life has been my guide?*
> *Heavenly peace, divinest comfort, here, by faith, in Him to dwell.*
> *For I know what e'er befall me, Jesus doeth all things well."*

I'm so thankful for the almost fourteen years of marriage the Lord gave me with Charles. The precious memories of serving the Lord together, raising and loving our eight children, praying together and loving each other will be cherished always. Charles loved our children and me with all his heart, but he loved his Lord most. His life was 100 percent dedicated to being a soldier of the King of Kings. He loved studying the crowns promised to those who are found faithful, and the last few months, he often talked to the boys about these crowns, and specifically, the martyr's crown. I remember him saying to all of us so many times what an honor and privilege it would be to give your life for your Savior and receive the martyr's crown! Though he was not desirous of death, he was desirous of every possible crown to cast at his Savior's feet!

Those twelve days the Lord gave us in Cameroon will always be treasured by our family. So many precious and special things the Lord allowed us to do and participate in! A major part of our family's heart is still in Cameroon. The love the Lord gave our family for the people there has not changed. Although we knew we had to leave, it broke our hearts to do so. Charles' heart was there, and he shed his blood for the people of that land. There are still so many who do not know the Savior. Charles would not want Christians to sit around and cry. He would tell them to live each day in light of eternity and to live as soldiers of the cross.

Many years ago our family made the choice of Joshua 24:15: "If it seem evil unto you to serve the LORD, choose you this day whom ye will serve, whether the gods which your fathers served that were on the other side of the flood, or the gods of the Amorites, in whose land ye dwell: but as for me and my house, we will serve the LORD."

By God's grace, and because He lives in us, our family, through His strength, will continue to serve the God our husband and daddy loved with all his heart. We desire that Jesus Christ will be lifted up and glorified always.

Revelation 4:11 says, "Thou art worthy, O Lord, to receive glory and honour and power: for thou hast created all things, and for thy pleasure they are and were created."

"May the Lamb that was slain receive the reward of His suffering."

To this Ben added his own words: "Charles Wesco esteemed others better than himself. He preferred obedience to Christ above his own safety and health. He loved the people of Cameroon more than his own comfort and ease. He loved the glorious gospel of Christ more than he loved his own life."

It was so encouraging to have many of the missionaries from Cameroon at the public memorial service. As a missionary family, we all joined our voices together and victoriously sang a song that has only become dearer to my heart with each passing day.

Great Is Thy Faithfulness

Great is thy faithfulness, O God my Father;
there is no shadow of turning with thee;
Thou changest not, Thy compassions, they fail not;
as Thou hast been Thou forever wilt be.

Chorus:

Great is thy faithfulness! Great is thy faithfulness!
Morning by morning new mercies I see:
all I have needed thy hand hath provided--
Great is thy faithfulness, Lord, unto me!

Summer and winter and springtime and harvest,
sun, moon, and stars in their courses above
join with all nature in manifold witness
to thy great faithfulness, mercy, and love.

Chorus:
Great is thy faithfulness! Great is thy faithfulness!
Morning by morning new mercies I see:
all I have needed thy hand hath provided--
Great is thy faithfulness, Lord, unto me!

Pardon for sin and a peace that endureth,
thine own dear presence to cheer and to guide,
strength for today and bright hope for tomorrow,
blessings all mine, with ten thousand beside!

—Thomas Chisholm, Public Domain

Pastor Randy King, who was in charge of our mission board and whom Charles had dearly loved and respected, preached the message. We closed the service with a song that held great significance for me as I look ahead. Years ago, it held significance for Jim Elliot and his four missionary companions before their martyrdom.

We Rest On Thee

We rest on Thee, our Shield and our Defender!
We go not forth alone against the foe;
Strong in Thy strength, safe in Thy keeping tender,
We rest on Thee, and in Thy Name we go.

Yes, in Thy Name, O Captain of salvation!
In Thy dear Name, all other names above;
Jesus our Righteousness, our sure Foundation,
Our Prince of glory and our King of love.

We go in faith, our own great weakness feeling,
And needing more each day Thy grace to know:
Yet from our hearts a song of triumph pealing,
"We rest on Thee, and in Thy Name we go."

We rest on Thee, our Shield and our Defender!
Thine is the battle, Thine shall be the praise;
When passing through the gates of pearly splendor,
Victors, we rest with Thee, through endless days.

—Edith G. Cherry, Public Domain

I was overwhelmed by the number of people who came to the service that day. Charles' life and death had impacted more people than I could have imagined, and because of his faithful testimony for the Lord in life, he had left behind a good name and glorified the Lord even in his death. The several hours after the service were spent greeting everyone in the long line of people who wanted to share their condolences. What a blessing it was to see how many people had been impacted by my husband. God gave me a precious reminder that day: you never know in your lifetime the full impact you have on those around you.

12

"WHY AM I HERE?"

The days following the funeral and memorial services went by in a blur. We were able to spend a day alone with the Sinclair family. We affectionately called our combined group the "Wesclairs!" Our time together was short but so needed as we all tried to build each other up and focus together on the faithfulness and goodness of our God. Uncle Ben and Aunt Becca got each of the kids something meaningful and special during that visit and did their best, even in the throes of their own upheaval and grief, to minister to us. Becca and I went out on a girl date together and had to laugh because so many people assumed, we were sisters. We were sisters, both in Christ and in understanding each other's messed up emotions and reactions to the trauma. When they left town, my heart broke all over again, feeling like the people I was closest to and who understood what I was going through were gone. The traumatic events that had bonded us together, causing us in many ways to feel like one big family, now caused us to have to separate geographically, and that was a hard reality to face.

So many aspects of life without Charles had to be faced right away. My parents had graciously opened up their home to us when we returned to the States. We were so thankful for a wonderful, safe place to live for those first two months. My sisters had done some research before we even got back, compiling a list for me of houses that would be possibilities for a home for us. I really struggled as we looked through the pictures. My cement-block house in Cameroon had been perfect. The Lord had truly given me complete and happy contentment in having very little, including virtually no electricity in the twelve days of living there. So many temporal things in life mattered so little to me now. None of the houses looked like something I would even be able to consider. But God was so good! After no success with her long list, my sister said, "Well, there was this one other one we saw . . ."

As soon as I looked at the pictures, I knew it was the one for us! It was a little older, the price was significantly cheaper, and the photos showed a house that I could easily picture being our home. My friend called the realtor and set up an appointment for us to see it the day before Charles' funeral. It had plenty of space, a great yard, and a layout that went above and beyond what I could have hoped for. Most importantly, my children loved it! The hand of God was clearly leading, and in the following weeks we went through the inspections and necessary paperwork. Thanks to some money Charles had saved as well as to God's provision through many people who gave sacrificially and beyond any level we could have imagined, we had the funds we needed to purchase the house in early December. It needed a really good cleaning and lots of painting as well as some other work. Over the next several weeks, my brother and sisters along with other family and many friends worked together to get the house ready for us to move into. We were thankful to be able to move in the first week of January and to finally have a place of our own to call home.

The holiday season of 2018 was hard. November 20, which would have been our fourteenth wedding anniversary, was an extra tough day to get through because it fell on the three-week anniversary of Charles' death. Memories from our wedding day mixed with flashbacks from three weeks earlier. That mess of jumbled emotions and thoughts made me feel like someone who was losing her mind.

During those early winter weeks, vivid nightmares and flashbacks were a regular part of my life throughout the day and night. Any sharp sound made my heart race and my body jump. I was terrified to ever leave my kids and had to force myself to get in a car and drive. I was so thankful for the Lord's protection from accidents because I found myself messed up multiple times when in a vehicle.

Throughout the Thanksgiving and Christmas season, many people reached out to our family in love, kindness, and generosity, constantly showering us with reminders of our heavenly Father's care for us. The children lived on the flow of cards and gifts sent from friends and brothers and sisters in Christ around the country. It warmed my heart to see them smile and be happy. We enjoyed spending the holidays with family and friends and were overwhelmed daily with reminders of God's goodness to us.

Christmas - 2018

To Die Is Gain

The last few months of 2018 did not play out in a way I would ever have dreamed or planned. From my human perspective, every realm of life was turned upside down, every hope dashed, every desire killed. Years of travel and ministry, hours of prayer and preparation for Cameroon, and twelve days of life in a third-world country seemingly wasted. But from the heavenly perspective of a God who does all things well, every aspect of this was part of a plan much bigger and greater than my human mind could imagine.

During those first eight weeks following Charles' death, one statement he had made throughout all of deputation kept me centered on Jesus—looking to Him and serving Him: "Living for eternity is always worth it!"

I closed out the hardest year of my life in darkness, trying to cover my ears so I wouldn't hear the fireworks and guns being fired to bring in the new year. I was curled up in a ball in bed, weeping and crying out to God simply for the strength to breathe and live and feeling like there was no hope of ever seeing happiness or light in life again. But I knew in my heart that my God was faithful. I knew His promises were true and that He had not forsaken me or my precious children. Even though I could see no hope or light at the end of the dark tunnel I was in, I knew that my Savior was holding my hand and asking me, in His still small voice, to trust Him in the dark. He had not made one mistake in His sovereign plan throughout 2018, and all I could do was trust Him to show Himself strong in 2019.

Moving into our new house was like a Band-Aid for all the hurt and trauma that filled my heart. I focused on turning the new house into a home, setting up the children's bedrooms and schoolroom, decorating, and trying to find the new "normal" for our family. It was special to begin having family devotions together again. Liberty came down weekly and spent time with us, and we all felt complete being together. With an unspoken bond between us, we somehow found comfort in just living life as a group. At the end of January, we all drove down to Tennessee, met up with the Sinclairs, and drove together from there to Southland Christian Camp in Louisiana for a few days of family camp with all the Cameroonian missionaries.

What a blessing it was to see everyone again! We all felt like a big family. No one had to try to put on an act of being strong. We all knew that we were struggling in our own ways, and there was such a precious spirit of love and unity in Christ as we sang together, heard encouraging preaching, and spent time fellowshipping and trying to build up each other so we could heal.

A pastor from Colorado was our camp speaker, and God used him to bring hope and encouragement to each of us that week. His spirit of love and kindness ministered to my heart, and I will be forever grateful for the way the Lord orchestrated his ministry to all of us. The last day was hard since many goodbyes had to be said as each family went their way, but many sweet and precious memories were made that week. Because of that camp, my PTSD was partially "Band-Aided" for a short time. God gave me some beacons of hope during those days with our Cameroonian missionary family.

Early on Tuesday morning of that week of camp, I woke up with a start at the same time I did every Tuesday those first few months—the time Charles was shot. But that Tuesday morning when I woke up, the Lord began flooding my heart with words. I quickly got up and began writing them down. It was like He was speaking them directly to me in a real and beautiful way. I honestly did not even feel the reality of some of the words at that point, but they were clearly flowing from God's heart to mine, giving me peace, hope, and comfort that morning.

> *My child, give Me your every expectation.*
> *Wait patiently on Me; My plan is best.*
> *Come unto Me and give Me your burdens.*
> *Trust in My love, and I'll give you rest.*
> *My ways are higher than you'll ever imagine.*
> *Watch Me fulfill your heart's every desire.*
> *Delight in My love; I never will leave you.*
> *Though the flame's hot, I'm here in the fire.*
> *I'm molding you into a vessel for service.*
> *My heart's one wish is to make you like Me.*

Become transformed into My image;
A living sacrifice I want you to be.
And then one day, when you stand before Me
Clothed in My righteousness, glorified—
Then you will know that your pain was worth it.
Eternally rest, content by My side.

—Stephanie Wesco

February brought new deep challenges as the pain in my back and abdomen began hitting me in waves. At times I could hardly move because it became more intense, but I tried to push through and keep living life. Having family devotions together consistently became very precious to me and the children. We would sing for a long time, read Bible stories, and pray together. God used those early days of family devotions to help keep our hearts and minds through Christ Jesus! We began learning a new song together—our first since Charles' death. "In Faith I Follow" so clearly described how we felt as a family and what the prayer of our heart was. That song became a nightly regular and was used by the Lord to bring comfort, healing, and strength to us spiritually. Physically, life was getting worse for me. Pain became a part of every moment, and good sleep became less frequent and hard to attain. Four or five hours felt like a really good night, with the norm being two to three hours.

Although I felt closer to God than ever before in my life, I really believed that God had set me on a shelf, never to use me again. This broke my heart because the only desire or purpose I had ever had in life was to serve Him. I did not understand what He was doing, and at times I found myself in hopeless despair, begging Him to still use me somehow, in some way that I could not yet see. I knew I was broken; I felt like a smashed, useless vessel beyond any hope of repair, but I cried out to God to heal and use me if it was still possible. As the nightmares and flashbacks caused me to fall deeper into a pit of hopelessness, the only thing I had to cling to and stand on was God's promises in His Word. Scripture journaling had become a part of my daily routine in January, and by February it was one of only two things keeping me from giving up on life. The other was caring for and trying to love and help my children, who were still dealing with so much grief and trauma of their own.

The week of Valentine's Day started off with new heartache when I received word that someone, I knew had committed suicide. The news sent me reeling. He had shot himself in the head, so just hearing about his death and how he died caused me to relive Charles' death. I found myself sitting in church that Sunday morning, unable to focus, unable to do anything except see blood. After the service, a lady said something to me that I will never forget when I told her how broken my heart was for the widow of the man who committed suicide: "Stephanie, you will be able to minister to her like no one else because you know the pain she is going through like no one else."

Visiting Daddy's grave on Valentine's Day - 2019

That statement stung like rubbing alcohol on an open wound! It caused me to recoil in my fleshly, selfish heart. I wanted so much to reach out to this sweet young widow, who I knew was grieving on a level I could not even begin to understand, but I did not want to identify with any of her pain. I did not want to be able to know or feel what she was going through. In my selfish flesh, I wanted to remain blissfully ignorant and not have to identify with her feelings of pain, loss, and suffering. What I did not see that day or even in the couple of weeks following was that God was going to use that horrific event and that young widow's need for someone as preparation for laying a new burden on my heart—His calling for my life—to give me hope and a future.

I forced myself to go to the funeral. It was another cold, blustery, and ice-coated day. Everything in me cried for a way out that morning as I drove to the funeral home. The room was packed with people; at the front was the closed casket. I sat in the back with some dear friends and looked around. The atmosphere was heavy with grief and shock. In contrast to Charles' funeral, where there had been a spirit of rejoicing in the Lord even amid the grief, this funeral exuded a spirit of loss and an almost hopelessness. As the widow got up to give a tribute in memory of her husband, God broke my heart for her. We had hardly ever interacted before that day. I watched her stand there without tears, trembling, her voice breaking as she told how much she loved and missed him. It was then that I knew God wanted me to reach out to her. I did not even know what that would look like, but I was sure that it was what God wanted me to do.

After the funeral and graveside service, everyone went to a local church, where a meal was being provided. As I walked into the ladies' room, I saw her standing at the sink, staring at herself in the mirror, her face full of shock. Her whole body was shaking. My mind raced back to the first time I looked in a mirror after Charles' death, and I saw my face again filled with that same shock, horror, and grief. I walked over to her and put my arm around her. She turned and almost collapsed in my arms, her body shaking like a leaf. She didn't cry. There were no tears, only broken words, as she poured out her heart to me. For the first time since Charles' death, God gave me a slight glimpse of one of His purposes for taking me through my deep valley of trauma, loss, and pain. As I stood there, one young widow trying to comfort and calm another, the Lord gave me a heavy burden I had not had up until that moment—a burden to help someone else whose heart had been completely broken like mine. I did not know how to do it, except by hugging her, empathizing as much as I could with her shock and trauma, praying with her, and then getting her something to eat and drink. God was beginning a new work in my heart that had not previously been there.

Over the next several weeks, I poured hours of prayer into my newly widowed friend, who needed to see the love and hope Jesus could give her. But I felt so clueless as to how to help her since her husband's death had triggered my own PTSD, causing my symptoms to intensify on a whole new level. How could I help someone else when I felt like I was drowning myself?

13

DROWNING

I will never forget that Sunday afternoon. After a horrific night of nightmares and a full morning at church, I lay down for a nap, completely exhausted. As soon as sleep came, I was hit a nightmare that was so bad that I woke up weeping and clinging to my pillow. That night after church, I went to my father/pastor and told him I had to get help. He told me he would look into finding someone who could help me.

Rhonda, Liberty's mom, is one of my very best friends in the whole world, and she knew that I was not doing well and needed help. She researched online and came across the website of a ministry called Wounded Spirits. After watching some of the YouTube video classes on different aspects of PTSD, she contacted Doug Carragher and explained the situation. She also gave the information about Doug and his PTSD counseling ministry to my dad. He called Doug, and in God's providence and mercy, Doug had time open to fly to Indiana and meet with me. Dad and Rhonda both told me about Doug's ministry, but I was very skeptical at first. Watching videos of him talking about flashbacks, nightmares, and triggers helped me, though. For the first time, someone understood and could accurately describe exactly what I was living with on a daily/nightly basis!

The first week of March began with Caleb's fifth birthday! I tried to do a fun birthday party for him with the family members and friends he wanted to invite. We had a great time together even though my pain level was extremely high throughout the evening. The next morning, I woke up with abdominal pain so bad that I was throwing up. It felt like something was seriously wrong, so I called my dad and told him. We thought it was probably appendicitis, so I dropped the children off at my parents' home and Dad drove me to meet with my doctor, who immediately sent us to the ER.

Once I was admitted, they drew labs, put me on an IV since I was dehydrated, and gave me a powerful narcotic. After a long wait, they came and took me for a CT scan. Later the doctor came in and told us that it was not my appendix. She thought I was dealing with irritable bowel syndrome and mentioned that they saw a lesion on my liver. She said not to give it a second thought since those are common and it did not concern them in the slightest. With that information, we returned to my doctor's office. During that visit, he told me he thought that much of what I was dealing with was indeed related to PTSD. He said the pain I was feeling was very common with PTSD. He also recommended an electroencephalogram to find out if signs of trauma showed up in my brainwave patterns. He told me about a special therapy that was available to help retrain the brain pathways after a person has been through trauma. We scheduled the test and went home, thanking the Lord that it was not appendicitis and knowing that my pain was simply a part of the horrid trauma package.

Saturday of that week was a bad day. I was dealing all day with an ongoing flashback that would not let go of my mind. The older boys needed new shoes, so we went to the store to get them, but even there, I could not shake it off. As we prepared to head for home, my dad said, "I picked Doug Carragher up at the airport. He likes to talk like Charles did! He told me the about one of the events in his life that led to his PTSD."

Dad then proceeded to give me a condensed version of the story. As soon as I heard the words, "He got the guy's blood in his mouth," I lost it. I told Dad I could not do counseling with Doug. I told him there was just no way I could open up and tell someone I did not even know all the horrible things I was feeling inside. My father calmly and sweetly responded by asking me to simply try talking to Doug. Since he thought it would help me, I told him I would try.

When Sunday morning came, I had a knot in my stomach. I had an image in my mind of what this PTSD counselor would be—stiff, non-caring, condescending, and judgmental. He would list all the ways I was failing God and everyone around me, and I would end up feeling worse than I already did. I smile now when I remember how scared I was to go into church that morning and meet the guy that was supposed to help "fix" me. I remember walking into the auditorium and seeing him standing near the front, looking like a giant, which caused my fear level to jump even higher!

When he got up to speak, everything he said made complete

sense. I could identify with all of it—except the part about *recovering* from the trauma and PTSD. It all made sense, though, and for the first time, I felt a twinge of hope for the possibility of healing in my heart. After Sunday school, Dad introduced Doug to me. Never would I have dreamed at that point that I had just met someone who would turn out to be one of the greatest friends a person could ever have.

Both sermons that day blessed and encouraged me so much. After church that evening my friends Steve and Rhonda Hicks and Doug came over. We had so much fun, and the kids loved him. He introduced us to the wonderful world of Marco Polo, the video chat application for cell phones, and the beautiful phrase, "Love you like a relative!"

As the evening came to a close, we made plans for him to come back to the house the following day for our first counseling session, while Rhonda and her girls took care of the children. When Monday morning dawned, there was a knot in my stomach again. What was it going to be like? How could I be honest with a stranger? Would he really understand? Would he confirm what I thought of myself—that I was messed up and something was wrong with me?

Doug walked in the door with a cup of Starbucks in his hand as friendly as could be. I was relieved! He hadn't become stiff—and he loved coffee. Both very good signs! After a short chat around the kitchen counter, Rhonda took the children, and we sat down in the family room. Though I am sure he initially said other things, the first words that I remember hearing were, "Stephanie, I just want to be your friend."

Sergeant Major Doug Carragher, US Army retired. He seemed intimidating at first.

At that moment, every wall I had built up to protect myself from this PTSD counselor fell down with a crash. Months after we first met for counseling, Doug shared his thoughts and notes from those first sessions. One of the first things I said to him was, "I want to dig a deep hole, hop in, and cover myself!" When he asked me if I had ever contemplated suicide, I responded with, "I will not kill myself! My kids need me!"

Nevertheless, Doug quickly figured out that suicide had crossed my mind as a possibility and spent that first session reinforcing things I already knew concerning how wrong suicide was. He asked me to tell him the story of Charles' death. Through that, he was able to understand in a whole new way why I was dealing with so many PTSD symptoms. He spoke about hope and about God using this trial in my life for His glory. Though I am not sure I appreciated all he said to me, I knew he was right. He encouraged me to keep going to the doctor to get help with the PTSD and constant pain that was still plaguing me.

I will always be so thankful to the Lord for the commitment Doug had to helping me himself instead of passing me off to some other counselor. I never would have dreamed that first day, that God had just given me one of the greatest gifts in the world—a friend who would stick closer than a brother. The other great thing about that first visit was a confirmed mutual love for Starbucks, which continues on to the present!

Meeting Doug

Our second and third days of counseling began the complex process of Doug seeking to unravel the reasons why I had no self-esteem and why, in many ways, I did not seem to even know who I was. He could see I loved my children and was wholly committed to loving and raising them, and yet I had no confidence or belief that I was capable of anything.

The second morning, he started going over the multiple symptoms of PTSD with me. Though anger, apathy, shame, and suicide were not things I was struggling with, many of the other painful realities of PTSD had become defining parts of who I was. The fear, anxiety, flashbacks, nightmares, pain, and a tremendous amount of survivor's guilt were consuming me. Doug asked me about my upbringing because in my responses to him he saw signs of my having been abused somehow. But after questioning me, he could tell that it had in no way come from my parents or home life. As he asked more about Charles and me, our marriage history, and our life together, he realized that there were many more layers of the onion that I was reluctant to peel off and share with him.

By the third day, Doug began to realize that there were very clear reasons for the symptoms of emotional, mental, and spiritual abuse I was showing. The abnormal Charles had been raised in, and which I had been around for so long, had in many ways become my normal too. As I tried to excuse and to explain away as normal many years of behavior that had clearly been abusive, God revealed to Doug that certain aspects of my PTSD were indeed being made much worse because of life experiences during my years of marriage. I had been living in a shell for a very long time.

On that last day of our talking together, God used this new friend to give me a beautiful first glimpse of how He planned to answer my cries to Him to let me serve Him again in ministry. I'll never forget Doug telling me that he thought my healing from PTSD was going to involve my helping others who were hurting. He was an encourager; he did not tear me down, criticize or make me feel that I could not do life. And for the first time in a very long time, I heard myself laughing —I found myself happy and okay with being alive. For the first time in months, I wanted to live not only for my kids but also for a purpose that God had in store for me.

Seven months after our first counseling session, during one of our late-night talks, Doug shared the words to a song he had written. The first three verses were a compilation of numerous statements I had made to him during those initial days. In the early morning hours, after our phone conversation, I sat down at the piano, and the music to "Light from Heaven" was born. This "song in the night" has become one of my favorites as I think about all God has done and continues to do.

A Light From Heaven

When darkness clouds your very soul
And light is hard to find,
The valley's deeper than ever before.
The world is passing you by.

Chorus:
There's a light from Heaven, that never dims.
The Hope of Glory—our eyes turn to Him.
The Savior is waiting to guide you through
And share abundant life with you!
You feel alone in a room of friends;
Your heart aches with questions of why.
You feel you are spinning out of control
And know you are going to cry.

Chorus

The road is hard; the day is long.
You sense there's no end in sight.
Rest eludes you at every turn;
You begin to question why.

Chorus

The path, now lit with Light divine,
Brings peace through His comfort and love.
He guides through valleys where darkness thrives
To a view of Heaven above!

Chorus

—Doug Carragher & Stephanie Wesco - © 2020

After those three days of counseling, I was so sad that our time had come to an end. I felt like I finally had some hope. One of the last things Doug told me (again) was that he thought my healing was going to involve my helping other people. For some reason, as the children and I said goodbye to him, I did not really expect that I would ever hear from him again. Having been betrayed by "friends" I trusted in the past, I still was not sure that he was really my friend, much as I desperately wanted it to be so.

Just two days later, I received a call from a lady who was terribly upset because her son's widow had become very depressed. "Can you go see her? Can you help her?"

Doug's words rang in my ears, but I felt helpless. How could I help her? I called my dad and asked him to call Doug for me to see if he had any suggestions. Within a few minutes, we were having our first of what would soon become hundreds of phone calls. Doug assured me that God would give me the words I needed when I got there and that I should just pray and trust the Lord to lead. Then he said he was sorry. Completely confused, I asked him why. He said he had started praying when he left our house that God would put a person in my life who needed help, but he was not expecting it to happen so soon. I laughingly told him, "So I have you to blame for this. Thanks a lot!"

As I drove to the young woman's house, I prayed, begging God to help me. I had never felt so helpless and incapable of helping another person in my entire life. What could I say or do to help her?

As we sat down to talk, my heart broke to see her suffering. She was so broken. I began quoting Scripture to her and praying with her. Then I got to watch God do His work as she began to calm down a little bit and talk to me. In those moments, God showed me something so beautiful: I was just a broken person, trusting God to do a miracle, to show Himself strong in my weakness, and to use me to help another broken person. That day I knew beyond a shadow of a doubt that God wanted me to help that sweet young widow and other women who were suffering. He would do it not because there was anything in me that was capable, mighty, or wonderful, but because my God is "able to do exceedingly abundantly above all" I had been asking or thinking (Ephesians 3:20). He is God and can choose to use us however He sees fit.

But God was preparing to take me through another testing of my faith.

14

COMPLETELY BROKEN

A week or so later, I got a call from my doctor's office, informing me that I needed to go in for an MRI of my liver. The doctor was concerned about the lesion that had shown up in the CT scan and thought I should have it double-checked. I called the hospital and was scheduled for a week later. That week was one of the longest of my life. I found myself consumed with worry and fear as I thought about the possibilities. The Lord clearly laid it on my heart the Sunday before the MRI that I should be anointed with oil and prayed over by the pastors and deacons of our church. I do believe, looking back, that God honored and blessed that step of obedience.

My MRI was early on a Wednesday morning. I was so thankful that one of my dearest friends was willing to get up extremely early and meet me at the hospital. We prayed together before I was taken back and prepped for the scan. Throughout the entire scan, I struggled to stay calm because all the sounds the machine made kept threatening to send me into flashbacks and a panic attack. When it was over, my friend took me to a coffee shop, where we just sat, did our nails, and talked. It was a sweet time of fellowship. Then I headed to the doctor's office for PTSD therapy and an IV treatment. When I got to the office, the receptionist informed me that my MRI results had already been sent to them. After my therapy was done and my IV had been hooked up, they called me back to see the doctor. As soon as he walked in the room, I knew something was wrong. He informed me that the lesion was nothing to be concerned about, but the MRI had shown other masses on my liver. He was greatly concerned about them and recommended that I see an oncologist for a PET scan. The news hit me hard, draining from my heart any hope that I had for a normal life. The doctor was kind and compassionate as he took my hands in his and, with tears in his eyes, told me he was so sorry. I went back to the IV room, and one of the sweet nurses who knew everything that had happened in my life came over and just stood beside me. I laid my head against her and cried. I truly felt in those moments that God had completely forsaken me. I even said, "What have I done to make God so angry with me?"

I finished my IV treatment and went out to my van. For only the second time since Charles had died, I found myself feeling suicidal. I called my dad and talked to him for a few minutes, but he was at a Bible conference with my two oldest sons and could not talk long. He prayed with me and tried to help me refocus on the Lord, but despair and hopelessness had taken control. This felt like the final straw. I called Doug next. "I'm drowning" were my first words to him. The words *tumor* and *cancer* were ones I had always dreaded hearing, and now I had just heard them both. I felt like my life was completely over, as if God did not love me or care about me. It was the lowest day of my life. Months of virtually no sleep, high stress, and being constantly emotionally drained had taken their toll. Now hearing that I had tumors was the final weight to cause me to feel like I was truly drowning.

Doug kept talking to me, trying to encourage me that God was in control. He said that liver tumors were treatable, that it might not be cancer, and that I could, under no circumstances, hurt or kill myself. He kept me from doing something very foolish. Over the next month, he and Debbie became one of God's greatest tools to encourage and stabilize me. We had 241 phone conversations during those thirty difficult days. Once again, God used them as an instrument of stabilization for me. I also talked with several of my dearest friends. All of them encouraged me to stay focused on the Lord, and I was so thankful for their steadfast love and friendship during those hours of hopelessness and despair. One good friend came over to my house that evening and made food for me and tried to encourage my heart in the Lord.

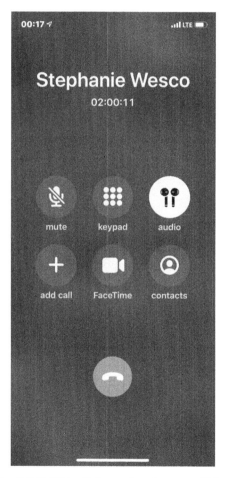

Doug"s & Debbie's cell phone—One of my many lifelines

The day I got the scan results, I was also introduced over the phone to one of God's greatest gifts to me—a woman who would soon become another of my very best friends, Doug's wife Debbie. I'll never forget her talking to me on the phone that day, trying to pump hope and courage into a heart that was tired and torn. She told me to not do any internet searches, to take something to help me sleep that night, to drink a large amount of water, and to trust God. She was sunshine to my day and brought a little smile back to my face a couple of times. I didn't even begin to realize then how much she would mean to me about ten days later.

The girls with Debbie - One of my dearest friends

Over the next few days, a friend worked hard to get my application in to a cancer treatment center as quickly as possible. I went on a detox diet, eating and drinking nothing but filtered water loaded with fresh lemon juice, freshly juiced organic veggies, cooked organic veggies, salad, organic eggs, avocados, cheese, and chicken. I was allowed to have an amazing tasting tea that became my coffee substitute as well as organic blueberries, so life felt pretty good. Due to the new meds and Emmy sleeping in her own bed for the first time since Charles' death, I began sleeping better. One day later that week, I realized my pain was slightly better. That greatly encouraged me.

At the same time the Lord brought me that week to new places of surrender that hurt in all new ways because I had to tell my precious children that I had tumors and didn't know what the future was going to look like. My heart broke as they went to stay at Grandpa and Grandma's house, five minutes away, so that I could rest and sleep. "God, what are you doing?" was the constant cry of my heart.

During those days, I buried myself in Scripture, pleading with the Lord to give me hope again in Him and in His promises to me. His Word came alive as I read and journaled the precious truths, He gave me. My Scripture journaling book became my "treasure chest!" That weekend, a friend came to spend a couple of days with me. She and I had a sweet time together that evening, talking through verses God was using in our lives to encourage and help us. Then she turned to 2 Corinthians 1:4 and read, "Who comforteth us in all our tribulation, that we may be able to comfort them which are in any trouble, by the comfort wherewith we ourselves are comforted of God."

She looked at me and said, "When I read this verse, I think of you, Stephanie. Many people have tried to help me, but you are the only one who has helped me get to know God better."

In that moment, tears filled my eyes as I thought of my faithlessness, despair, and hopelessness just a few days earlier. I realized anew how merciful and great my God was, that in my weakness and utter failure to stand strong on His promises, He was still choosing to use my brokenness to glorify Himself.

God also opened the door to a new facet of ministry that I had never anticipated. Doug had mentioned to me the night before that he had written lyrics for a song. There was no music, and it didn't even have a title yet. I had told him about a couple of songs I had written in the past and asked him to send the lyrics to me to look at, so he did. That Sunday evening, I began working on a few changes to the lyrics to help them flow and rhyme. Then I sat down at the piano, and the Lord quickly gave a melody. It was then that the song "The Holy Hill" was born. It was our first "song in the night," a gift from the Lord in the middle of a deep trial. It took my heart and mind off my problems and placed my focus on my Savior's love for me.

The Holy Hill

There was darkness that day on that holy hill
Where our Savior was crucified:
A physical sign of a sin-cursed world,
One without a clue of why.

Chorus:
Why would my Savior leave His throne,
Leave it for you and for me?
Why in the world would I stay and not serve
A Savior with that love for me.
There was pain that day on that holy hill;
The pain was for you and for me.
He took God's wrath and stood in our stead
So that pain would be history.

Chorus

There was thirst that day on that holy hill—
A thirst none has ever known.
He drank of the cup and paid sin's price
The depth of His love to show.

Chorus

There was death that day on that holy hill.
Young and old can have new destiny
For Christ crushed the serpent and conquered the grave.
There is life in eternity.

Chorus

*There was victory on that holy hill—
Greatest victory of eternity.
None can fully fathom the work of the cross:
Grace poured out at Calvary.*

—*Doug Carragher & Stephanie Wesco - © 2020*

Doug came to visit Tuesday afternoon of that week and brought a new round of encouragement, smiles, and laughter to our house. He also brought with him a good friend of his, Pastor Stephen Ashmore, and we sang the new song together. The Hicks were at our house that evening as well as another couple, who had come to help with the children, so they didn't always have to be away from me. It was a great evening of stories, laughter, and singing. I learned that Doug had an incredible gift as a storyteller, and it was wonderful to get a big medicinal dose of "a merry heart!" While they were there, Doug booked an airline ticket for Debbie to come out to Indiana to go with me to the cancer treatment center. Our family loved the time we were able to spend together, and I began to realize that the friendship God was giving all of us was going to be extra special.

Stephen Ashmore with Doug

The Lord laid it on Doug's and Debbie's hearts to start a special page on Facebook called "Praying for Stephanie Wesco." He began posting updates about what was going on with my health and asking for prayer. The response was overwhelming as brothers and sisters in Christ from around the world began praying for a miracle.

The next few days were filled with trying to rest and focus on God. I also went to my doctor's office for IV treatments. Those heavy doses of vitamin C made me feel much better. When Dad and I arrived home Friday afternoon, we got to meet Debbie for the first time. Weighing less than a hundred pounds and standing four feet eleven inches, she's small but strong and energetic. I knew immediately we were going to be great friends.

The next day we packed all the children's things that they would need for a week since it looked like I would be at the cancer center that long. Debbie was busy keeping all the children in line, making sure they weren't overpowering Mom with questions before they went over to my parents' home to stay for a while. Saturday evening, I tried to relax, not knowing what the following week would bring. I was prepared for cancer and the fact that I was going to have to fight for life. Sunday morning, Debbie and I went to church together even though I felt sick. My feelings told me that it was the cancer taking over. But Debbie kept reminding me of the positives in life and of things that pointed to the possibility of it not being cancer. She was my ray of sunshine during those days. Sunday afternoon I said goodbye to my family and my children. I wept, wondering what I would have to tell them the next time I saw them. We prayed together again for God's deliverance, and then Debbie and I headed home. I tried to rest some that afternoon and worked a little bit on music for my sister's upcoming wedding, but playing made my pain level spike, so that was a short-lived activity. We packed and prepared to leave the following morning for the cancer treatment center in Zion, Illinois. Rhonda was going to meet us there.

After checking in on Monday, I had exams and blood tests and was scheduled for a PET scan on Tuesday and a biopsy on Wednesday. After supper Debbie, Rhonda, and I drove to our hotel for the night. So many thoughts raced through my head that evening. One moment I would feel like I was completely at peace and the next moment like the turmoil inside was bubbling over. We had a time of prayer together and then went to bed, knowing that it would be an early Tuesday morning. Before going to sleep, I chose to read the five Psalms for the day. Because it was April 8, I read Psalm 8, 38, 68, 98, and 128. Through that Bible reading, the Lord showed Himself so real to me and flooded my heart in those moments with the peace that passes all understanding. The following verses all made their way into my Scripture journal that night as once again God made His Word a lamp to my feet and a light to my path:

> "For in thee, O LORD, do I hope: thou wilt hear, O LORD my God. . . . Forsake me not, O LORD: O my God, be not far from me. Make haste to help me, O Lord my salvation." ~Psalm 38:15, 21-22
>
> "But let the righteous be glad; let them rejoice before God: yea, let them exceedingly rejoice. Sing unto God, sing praises to his name: extol him that rideth upon the heavens by his name JAH, and

rejoice before him. A father to the fatherless, and a judge of the widows, is God in his holy habitation." ~Psalm 68:3-5

"The LORD shall bless thee out of Zion. . . . Yea, thou shalt see thy children's children." ~Psalm 128:5-6

Some may say that it was mere coincidence that I read those verses that night, but every day of life from October 30 and going forward had clearly shown me that I did not serve a God of coincidences, but a God who knows what we need and exactly when we need it. It was no accident in my mind that here I was, at a cancer treatment center in Zion, Illinois, and God gave me that promise from Psalm 128 to give me hope for the future! With these verses resting in my heart, I went to sleep.

Sometime around 5:00 a.m., I woke up startled. It was still completely dark outside, and I could see the moon as I stared out the window. The reality of where I was and what I was potentially facing that day sank in, along with my brain's Tuesday morning routine of nightmarish flashbacks and memories. I lay there crying out to God for help, for strength, for a miracle. My unbelieving, sinful flesh told me that God didn't care. I had begged for a miracle that fateful October Tuesday, many weeks before, and God didn't care then. So why would He care now? My wicked, deceitful heart said that He had let Charles die and He was going to just let me die too. I could not trust Him or His promises.

But then a still, small voice began breaking through the din of my noisy soul. He told me that His promises were true, that He was in control, and that He loved me with an everlasting love. He said He was never going to leave me or forsake me. He promised me that He was going to work all these things together for my good. He asked only one thing of me that morning. Just as the disciples were in the middle of a storm on the Sea of Galilee, in a sinking boat and fearing for their lives, I was in a sinking boat of PTSD and physical sickness, in the middle of a very real storm. He asked me to, by faith, get out of the boat, trust Him, and come to Him in the middle of the storm. I could see Him there, holding out His hand to me, asking me to trust Him. I told Him that I would sink, that I would fail, that I couldn't do it. He assured me that He was faithful and that nothing could take me out of His hand. He told me He knew I couldn't do it on my own but told me that I could do it through Him because He was my strength. He told me to keep looking to Him and just take one step at a time. Through tears, there in the quiet darkness, I told Him I would trust and obey. That morning I chose, in a whole new way, to get out of my boat, which in reality was already sinking, and to come to Him through the storm.

As we continued in fellowship, He reminded me of the story of the woman who came to Jesus, having been sick for more than twelve years with an issue of blood. She had spent all her resources, and she came to Jesus seeking His healing power and knowing that He was able. As Jesus walked by her, she reached out and simply touched the hem of His garment. Immediately she was healed. As the story played through my mind, I knew what Jesus was challenging me to do. And there, in those early morning hours, I said to my Savior, "Lord, I am choosing to cling to the hem of Your garment, and I won't let go until You heal me!" The peace of God flooded my heart once again as I chose to trust Him.

We got up, got ready, and headed back to the hospital for the ominous PET scan. Debbie was a nurse, and because of her expertise, she had the foresight to request a mild sedative for me to help prevent any panic attacks and claustrophobia during the scan. I took it right before the technician came to get me from the waiting room. I cannot say enough about the gentle kindness that was shown to me that morning. The technician was so gracious and thoughtful as he went through the preparation process, gave me the injections, and carefully explained what the scan would do. He then led me to a room to relax and wait for the injection to take effect. As I lay there waiting, the Lord flooded my heart with His promises. I wondered what parts of me were going to light up. Was there going to be cancer in other places besides the liver? Though there was still a sense of fear that I could not seem to escape, I kept choosing to believe His promises.

Finally, the technician came and led me into the room for the scan. The medicine was beginning to work, so I was a little unstable on my feet. He got me situated on the table, explained the process, and left the room. Debbie had told me to close my eyes before the scan and not to open them till it was over, so I did. Soon I was moving into the machine. At first, a wave of fear washed over me, and all I knew to do at the moment was choose to keep my feet anchored on the rock of God's promises. In a few moments, I experienced something I *never* want to forget. It literally felt like God took every single ounce of fear out of my body and replaced it with calming grace and peace that I had never known before that moment. I had *no* fear. I had no "feeling" of being healed, and it wasn't like some fanciful magic. It was simply God keeping His promise to give a spirit of power, of love, and of a sound mind. I lay there rejoicing, knowing beyond a shadow of a doubt that my God was right there with me during the scan and that He was in complete control.

Once the scan was completed, the technician took me by wheelchair out to Debbie and Rhonda in the waiting room. The medicine had done its job, and my ability to walk in a straight line was a bit hampered, causing some laughs from my friends later that morning, much to my chagrin. The wheelchair proved to be a great blessing after I was able to walk again because it served as a great way to carry all of our purses, bags, and water bottles.

After breakfast, we tried to schedule a massage for me, thinking it might help relieve some of the pain, but we found out that when your body has radiation in it, massages aren't allowed. So much for that brilliant plan! Instead, we found a comfy area to sit and try to relax. Then a nurse, called to inform me they had the results from the PET scan and to confirm the details for my biopsy the following morning. My heart sank again because I understood her to say that they had found cancer. I asked her how much they had found, to which she replied it would just be a small spot that needed the biopsy. Her response was vague, but it was enough to send me spiraling downward. Looking back, I am so very thankful for the friends who were there with me. They quickly began refocusing me, and we prayed together again, asking God to work. If God was teaching me anything, it was that surrender to and trust in Him are often moment-by-moment decisions of the heart.

That afternoon, we walked into the waiting room of the liver specialist, waiting to hear the official report from the PET scan. Having cancer was no longer a question in my mind, it was just a matter of know how much was there. Soon we were called back to meet with the doctor. I will never forget him walking into the room and saying, "I have some good news for you. I do not think you have cancer!"

Selfie: Rhonda Hicks, Debbie & me - REJOICING!

My head spun, and I did not believe him! I stuttered and stammered in disbelief as I questioned him about the phone call about the biopsy, I had received just a little while before. He told me he would check with the radiologists again. The wait for him to return seemed like an eternity. Finally, he reentered the room, smiling. "I have consulted with two different radiologists, and they both agree, you do not have cancer! Not one spot on your entire body lit up. You do not have any cancer!"

My heart was overwhelmed in those moments with thankfulness, joy, and still a large measure of disbelief. The doctor told me they were not sure what had caused the tumors, and without the biopsy, what they were made of. But he did not think we needed to do a biopsy since there was no sign of cancer. Then he questioned me about some other health issues, which he thought might have contributed to the liver tumors and told me they would want to see me in three months for another MRI to keep an eye on the tumors. Debbie and I went back to the waiting room, where Rhonda sat waiting. As we told her what the doctor had said, we all started crying, our hearts overflowing with gratefulness to our God for answering prayer. There had been thousands of believers around the world, begging God for a miracle, and God answered those prayers!

We had another doctor's appointment on the schedule, and as we went, we rejoiced in God's goodness. I called my dad and told him the good news. Before long, we were called back to meet with the initial nurse and doctor we had seen our first day there. With smiling faces they confirmed the news that there was no cancer. He also told me that my blood work looked really good. We were all rejoicing together, and as we walked out of the office, Debbie was so excited that she started doing the happy dance. Nurses were cheering, and there was a definite spirit of joy in the air. God had shown Himself strong, and now we got to praise Him publicly for what He had done.

That evening Rhonda went home, while Debbie and I stayed the night. I marveled at all God had done in that twenty-four hours. I stood in awe of the way He had shown Himself strong and steadfast. When I had been faithless, He was still faithful; when I had been weak, He had been strong; and when I had chosen to trust Him, He had once again shown Himself trustworthy! Several different passages from Psalms perfectly expressed my heart that night!

> "And they that know thy name will put their trust in thee: for thou, LORD, hast not forsaken them that seek thee. Sing praises to the LORD which dwelleth in Zion: declare among the people His doings." ~Psalm 9:10-11

> "I waited patiently for the LORD; and he inclined unto me, and heard my cry. He brought me up out of an horrible pit, out of the miry clay and set my feet upon a rock, and established my goings.

> And he hath put a new song in my mouth, even praise unto our God: many shall see it, and fear, and shall trust in the LORD. Blessed is the man that maketh the LORD his trust, and respecteth not the proud, nor turn aside to lies. Many, O LORD my God, are thy wonderful works which thou hast done, and thy thoughts when are to usward: they cannot be reckoned up in order unto thee: if I would declare and speak of them, they are more than can be numbered."
> ~Psalm 40:1-5

Before the initial MRI that revealed the tumors, I had heard a message from the passage in 1 Peter 1 on trials being a gift from God. I had really struggled with that concept although I knew it was true. But the evening after learning I did not have cancer but still multiple liver tumors that had to be monitored, I went back and read, and it struck me anew that this trial of my faith was a way God was seeking to bring praise and glory to Himself, and in light of eternity, that made my suffering worth it.

> "Wherein ye greatly rejoice, though now for a season, if need be, ye are in heaviness through manifold temptations: That the trial of your faith, being much more precious that of gold that perisheth, though it be tried with fire, might be found unto praise and honour and glory at the appearing of Jesus Christ: Whom having not seen, ye love: in whom, though now ye see him not, yet believing, ye rejoice with joy unspeakable and full of glory." ~1 Peter 1:6-8

We headed for home Wednesday morning. Instead of facing a biopsy, all I had to face was driving through Chicago traffic. The children were so excited. I remember Stephy's sweet hug and smile as she said happily, "You don't have cancer!"

15

REGROUPING

The following days were spent regrouping and finding ways to relieve stress since it had been determined that stress was one of the main causes of my ongoing pain. Following doctor's orders, we tried to change some things in life. One change was my going on a very strict diet. During this time, I was also so thankful for my true and faithful friends and counselors, who believed in me and began encouraging and building me up in so many different realms of life, where I previously had viewed myself as unable or incapable. With their patient help and teaching, I began to learn and grow in different ways, where Charles had totally been in charge before, but now it was up to me to take over for our family. As the healing process continued, the Lord used my dad, the Hicks, and the Carraghers to help me realize that different forms of trauma and abuse from years past had messed up my view of who I was before God. After having been told pointblank and in roundabout ways that I was "incapable of thinking for myself," I did not think I was capable. During the following weeks, I discovered that healing sometimes involves hurt as God revealed situations in my life that had to change little by little. He faithfully guided along each winding path. I continued to learn day by day and moment by moment that I could go to Him with everything and trust Him to lead.

Doug once texted to me when I was in the middle of attitude and mindset change: "They used to say in the Army that 'your attitude determines your altitude.'" It's true. My whole perspective on life was being altered—for the better! God had shown Himself strong. As the children and I incorporated new plans to help life move forward, including a teacher (my amazing sister-in-law, with whom I just happen to share the same name) to help with the younger children's schooling, and prepared for upcoming doors of ministry that God was opening, all I could do was come before Him daily with a heart overflowing with gratefulness and praise for all He was doing. He was making a way for us to walk through the valley, and He was showing us that He was our loving shepherd and guide.

Good Friday was a very exciting day because "The Holy Hill" was released on the public Facebook page. We watched God begin to use it to bless others. Another big step forward during this month was selling the motorhome that had been our home on the road through the years of deputation. There were many memories wrapped up in its walls. My heart broke the last time I walked through it alone. As memories flooded my mind of all the times we had spent traveling, talking together about Cameroon, and dreaming of our life there, I once again I had to surrender to God's plan being different from mine.

Doug and Debbie began seriously encouraging me to write a book about the story of our lives, Charles' martyrdom, and what God was doing. I was a bit scared and overwhelmed at the thought but began to seriously pray about whether it was God's will. At that point, I did not feel there was any strength or ability in me to write. At the end of April of 2019, a new phase of ministry began for us. We travelled for a month to several churches that had asked us to come to sing as a family and me to speak for ladies' groups. While we were at a mission's conference at a supporting church in Ohio, God used a message I heard about the testimony of the widow from Zarephath to confirm in my heart that He did indeed want me to write.

Our travels during those weeks took us to Ohio, Michigan, and our first Wounded Spirits PTSD Camp at Camp Joy in Whitewater, Wisconsin. That week was life changing for me in many respects as I learned more about how to counsel and help those suffering from different versions of trauma and the effects of PTSD.

Doug, Debbie and me

My thirty-fourth birthday happened to land during that week of training, and Doug and Debbie went out of their way to make it so special for me. My day started with a fresh "five pumps, extra hot, no water" Starbucks chai, along with "Happy Birthday" being sung outside my cabin door. What could be better than that? Brother John

O'Malley was there throughout the week, focusing on ministering to my children, and he quickly became their best friend. He took them shopping, and they got me a beautiful necklace and sweet cards. Doug, Debbie and their friend Harold Pierce had arranged for cakes and candles for suppertime, and by the time the day was over, I knew that God had blessed me more richly than I ever deserved. Having my eight precious children and the sweetest and most awesome friends in the world around me, I was so extremely blessed!

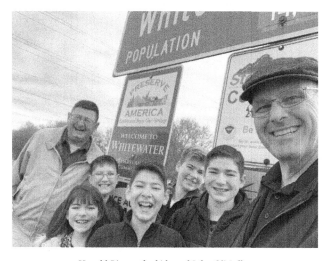

Harold Pierce, the kids and John O'Malley

Though it had been discussed briefly beforehand, it was during that week of camp that the Lord began to heavily impress on my heart as well as on the hearts of those connected with Armed Forces Baptist Missions and Wounded Spirits that God was leading our family to join AFBM's Wounded Spirits counseling ministry. Over the next several weeks, I prayed and sought counsel, wanting God's clear direction. At every turn, He clearly opened the doors, and I spent the last week of May preparing for my interview with board members of Armed Forces Baptist Missions. They voted to accept our family as part of their mission board. It was an exciting but bittersweet time for me as I thought back to 2015, when Charles and I had initially met with the leadership of First Light Baptist Mission and had begun the process of working through all the multiple details needed to prepare for deputation to go to Cameroon.

Now less than four years later, I was going through a similar process with a new mission board for a new ministry calling, alone. I knew beyond a shadow of doubt that God was working out His plan, but so many puzzle pieces did not fit in my mind yet. I was so thankful for all of the help we received from my dad, Doug, Debbie, Pastor Ashmore, the leadership of First Light Baptist Mission, our assistant pastor, my uncle, and others who aided us in the transition and preparation of a new family picture and prayer card, table display, prayer letter design, and numerous other aspects that were all new territory for me to face alone.

Throughout May and June, I was overwhelmed as the Lord began to expand the counseling ministry, regularly bringing across my path women who needed help and encouragement. I didn't have anything new, special, or unique to share with them—just Jesus, His love, and His promises. But I quickly discovered how many desperately needed just that. Many times, I felt so down myself and kept trying to back out of writing this book. But Doug found a verse that he thought would keep me under enough pressure from God to write.

Our correspondence went like this:

Stephanie: "I don't think I am up to writing this book!"

Doug: "Your book verse: 'Thus speaketh the LORD God of Israel, saying, Write thee all the words that I have spoken unto thee in a book.' (Jeremiah 30:2)."

Stephanie: "Of all the verses in the Bible, you had to find that one!"

Early in July, Debbie and I went back to the cancer center for follow-up blood work and an MRI on my liver. The Lord once again showed Himself strong because the liver specialist, reported to me that the tumors had not grown, and he told me to "go home and live life!" This was wonderful news and resulted in another happy dance from Debbie and me. God had answered prayers once again.

Debbie and me at the Cancer Treatment Center

The end of July brought an exciting event for our family—our first family camp with AFBM at Camp Joy. Liberty went with us, and we were all very excited. But as we drove that Monday, there was a cloud hanging over me because Tuesday would be the nine-month anniversary of Charles' death. For whatever reason, this anniversary was hitting me really hard. That evening, I struggled inside, every part of me wanting to rewind nine months and change the outcome of Charles' last twenty-four hours. Wasn't there some way to go back and redo? Wasn't there a way to be able to go back to living with no panic attacks, flashbacks, and nightmares? Wasn't there a way to escape the aching pain that filled my heart?

Fun times eating with Uncle Doug

After the children went to bed that night, my heart broke on a level it hadn't broken in a long time. The memories and loneliness hit like a flood. Doug and Debbie kept calling and texting, and I kept ignoring him. I did not want to talk. But finally, I called him back and opened up about what was going on in my heart. They knew my heart was hurting that night in a very deep way. I will forever be grateful for their willingness to pour into me when I felt completely empty. That night was the hardest I had faced since the day I initially found out about the liver tumors. I truly believe there was a spiritual battle going on in my heart because God knew what He wanted to do in my life that week, and the devil was doing all in his power to stop it.

Tuesday morning came quickly, and as we prepared to go to breakfast, there was a knock at the door. When I opened it, there stood Doug and Harold, holding—you guessed it—a Starbucks chai! Doug asked if I was OK, and even though I wasn't sure, I told him I was. Throughout that day, I sat in a daze at times, my mind wandering to nine months before, but really not wanting to rewind anymore, just having to helplessly watch it replay in my head. "God, I don't understand!" my heart uttered more than once that day. I kept remembering sitting through candidate training with First Light

Baptist Mission in 2016, with Charles sitting beside me. I remembered our excitement, our interaction with other missionaries who were there, our hopes, our plans, our goals. They had all been so good. They had all been for the purpose of seeing souls reached with the gospel. And yet, here I sat alone, starting over in a new ministry with a new mission board with a new purpose—excited yet struggling.

A gift from Heaven

God saw those struggles throughout that Tuesday, and I will never forget the message that Pastor Tom Hunter brought that evening about the life of Joseph. As he preached, the Lord began to do a whole new level of healing and putting puzzle pieces in place in my heart. I cannot even put into words exactly what God did, but as Pastor Hunter preached, the Lord opened my eyes to beautiful truths that helped me realize every single thing that God had allowed and orchestrated throughout the years Charles and I were together, the joys, victories, the broken dreams, the heartbreaks, even his death, were a part of His present plan to use me and the children in this new ministry. All the ways Charles and I had dreamed together of serving the Lord had *not* been fulfilled from my human viewpoint, but I realized on a whole new level that from God's point of view He *had* given us our dream come true—serving God together our entire marriage and, for Charles, being given the privilege of giving his life for his Lord. As with Joseph, Charles had chosen numerous times throughout his life to keep his focus and love fixed on His God in spite of the awful things people did to him. Through it all, he had chosen to stay faithful to God and true to his godly convictions. Like Joseph, he had kept his good name. After Charles' death, God began using his life and testimony as a legacy of living a life surrendered wholly to Jesus Christ. Now God is using it around the world to glorify Himself and spread the gospel farther than Charles ever could have in his lifetime. I realized that God had freed him in his death from pain, hurt, betrayal, and everything else in this sin-filled world. I also realized during that message that God was giving me a special part in this ongoing story. He was giving me the job of carrying on where my husband left off—to continue sharing the love of Jesus, and the hope He gives, not only with the lost who are hurting but also with believers who are suffering.

Pastor Hunter pointed out something I will never forget. He said that if Joseph had not chosen to see all that God had allowed in his life as part of God's plan for him and had stopped trusting God, he never would have ended up fulfilling God's ultimate plan for his life as the governor of Egypt who saved the world from a famine. That statement hit hard and quickly soaked into my heart and mind. I knew in those moments that God's ultimate plan for my life was where He had placed me now—not in Cameroon, though part of my heart would always be there—as part of this mission board and this ministry, helping people who need the hope and help only God and His Word can give. As God opened my eyes to these wonderful truths, peace and joy filled my heart, and I knew that the pain I had experienced was not in vain. I knew that, just as in the life of Joseph, in my life God's unseen hand had been at work. Many times, He allowed things that seemed so useless at the time to help prepare me for His plan. It left me feeling as if I had been freed in a whole new way from a prison. In my heart I knew I could say with a smile to anyone who had tried or might still try to hurt me: "Ye thought evil against me; but God meant it for good, to bring to pass, as it is this day, to save much people alive" (Genesis 50:19–20).

Tom Hunter preaching

My responsibility before God was clear. It was to choose to embrace God's good and perfect plan for me and the children moving forward. I had to choose to lay aside weights and hopeless, unresolvable, energy-sucking situations in life, so that I would be able to run with patience the race God had set before me. By doing so, I would see God work in more amazing ways than I could ever imagine. And almost more importantly, I was to choose to calmly and joyfully rest in the fact that God's good and perfect plan had been accomplished in Charles' life and through his death—to let him go, not forgetting him or his part in my life, but to move forward in new ways, looking to Jesus as my vision and guide for the future.

That night found my heart filled with the peace and joy it hadn't known in a long time. Doug, Debbie, and I rejoiced together as the light bulbs they had been trying to install in my brain finally turned on. It was another step forward and new level of healing.

The next day, God introduced another realm of thinking that needed to be changed in my life. Pastor Hunter preached a message specifically to the women of the mission board about the important role they play in the church and ministry. He stressed the importance of women not losing their personal identity in the Lord and who He has made them to be. He used the story of Abigail, the wife of Nabal, as an example of a woman who loved God and did what was right before God even though her husband was an ungodly, churlish man. As he preached, my brain began swirling. I felt like I was being hit with a form of culture shock. Throughout my years of marriage, I had been engulfed in a very different belief system about a woman's position and role in life. As a result, it almost struck me as wrong to view women such as Abigail, Esther, and Deborah as heroes even though I believed God did hold them up in Scripture as such. Now to be hearing preaching that encouraged women to have an identity and courage and that treated them with this level of respect and dignity struck me as almost foreign.

Pastor Hunter was very understanding of my "culture shock" reaction, and it was a blessing to be able to talk with him later and begin to clarify my thinking. It was freeing in so many ways to realize that God viewed me as someone of great value who didn't need to try to fit into anyone else's mold or preplanned agenda for me—as someone He wanted to use in ministry and service for His glory.

The rest of the week brought many special moments as our AFBM family was drawn closer to each other and the Lord. One evening, the Lord opened up a counseling opportunity that resulted in my getting to work with Doug and Debbie in a new way. It was a gift from the Lord as I realized how much God was doing in our lives and ministry together.

New partners in the ministry

On a funny note, God used five-year-old Caleb, who has no shame, to provide a whole new level of "real" for our family. One morning when Doug and an AFBM board member arrived with the daily supply of Starbucks, Caleb, who had been complaining of an itching problem, wanted to show Uncle Doug his issue. Right then with no second thought, he dropped his drawers, pointed at his rear end, and said, "Uncle Doug, look!" It was evident that he had sat on anthill the evening before, and fire ants had bitten him. I was too embarrassed to be concerned about his bites. Doug, while doubled over laughing, quickly diagnosed the problem and assured Caleb that Aunt Debbie had cream that would help fix the itching. Caleb was happy with the solution. Later in the day, with no shame, he yelled across the dining hall, "Uncle Doug, I don't itch anymore!"

A familiar scene at camp - with Uncle Doug

My happy family - Camp Joy, Wisconsin

Those days with our new AFBM family were so treasured because the Lord gave us a special bond with the other missionary families and board members who were there. The children and I loved watching the Lord bless us with yet another part of the mission's family He had started giving us way back when we began the journey to Cameroon.

At the close of that week, we traveled for the first time with the Carraghers to a meeting. The pastor had requested that I share the testimony of Charles' martyrdom and what transpired in Cameroon. This was a first for me, and Saturday night as I went to bed, I cried out to the Lord for help. Nothing in me wanted to relive or retell the story, so I asked the Lord to give me the words He wanted me to say and to use it for His honor and glory. Otherwise, there was no purpose to the pain. Sunday morning came, and as Sunday school began, I kept bringing my same request to the Lord.

In response to my cries for help, the Lord showered His promised all-sufficient grace on me. The pain was still indescribable and the memories still horrific, but God's grace and strength were even greater. Truly, His strength was made perfect in my weakness. Even though I had not asked the Lord for any fruit that morning, seeing the response of young people to the testimony of what God had done and was doing astounded me. What an incredible reminder it was to stay faithful and trust God to work all things together for my good and His glory. After seeing God use that first time of sharing the story of Charles' martyrdom with a church, God gave me another gift amid grief—seeing Charles' life purpose being fulfilled even in his death. I knew at that point, that one of the reasons God wanted me to keep telling the story, was to carry on Charles' whole purpose for living— to motivate a deeper love for God and His Word in the life of every person with whom he came in contact.

The following months brought continued healing as God kept reminding me that He wanted me to focus on others' needs more than my own. When women would contact me seeking help or encouragement, some counseling sessions (whether via text, phone call, or in person) would leave me prostrate before the Lord, crying out to Him for help to help others, asking Him to do great and mighty healing in the precious lives of women who had been through so much heartache.

In August of 2019, God opened the door to some meetings in the South. We had so much fun driving down to meet up with the Carraghers and heading to a mission's conference in Georgia together. After the kids were put to bed that evening at Doug and Debbie's house, we sat in the living room, working on computer work. Doug started throwing out words to a new song the Lord had put on his heart. We talked it through and formulated the verses and chorus. Before that evening was over, our next song was written. "Fear Not, My Child" would get its music a few days later while we were in Georgia. The words are beautiful; they perfectly reflect what we and so many others who have dealt with trauma and PTSD experience as well as the healing that God does. I was reminded again of the sweetness God seeks to give us as we try to "make a well in the valley" for others to draw from in their need.

Fear Not, My Child

Sometimes I wake with pain and fear of dying.
It hurts so bad, no answers here to find.
But then I hear my Savior softly speaking,
"Trust Me, My child! I'm right here by your side."
Chorus:
Fear not, My child! I've walked the path you're walking.
Fear not, My child! I'll carry you along.
Fear not, My child, and trust in Me, Eternal!
Your faith's reward, your comfort, and your song.

Chorus
I daily search for answers to my problems.
My searches end with emptiness and pain.
But Jesus died and granted my full pardon,
So now I bow and call upon His name.

Chorus
I've found my joy, my strength, my hope, my healing,
Sufficient grace, abundant in supply.
And now to Christ, my Savior, I am clinging.
I'll live for Him and serve Him till I die.

Chorus

—Doug Carragher & Stephanie Wesco - © 2020

"O sing unto the LORD a new song: sing unto the LORD, all the earth." ~Psalm 96:1

"I will sing a new song unto thee, O God: upon a psaltery and an instrument of ten strings will I sing praises unto thee." ~Psalm 144:9

Performing "Fear Not, My Child" for the first time

I was seeking to help women, but in addition the Lord began making it clear that as part of this ministry He was giving songs to help people. The Lord gave Doug "Steadfast in Trials" after the PTSD camp in May 2019, when I was struggling through the many emotions of the nine-month anniversary. But Doug did not show it to me till later that year. It was such a blessing, and the Lord graciously gave music to go with it in a very short time.

Steadfast in Trials

Our trials of faith in this life are constant.

They hurt so bad, we often lose our way.
In this world we will face tribulation,
But take heart and trust in Christ today.

Chorus:
Steadfast in trials! Rejoice in hope—be patient.
Steadfast in trials! Be constant in prayer.
Steadfast in trials! Keep looking unto Jesus!
Steadfast in trials! Your burden He will bear.
When we are tired and feeling weak and frail,
Our days seem long, and we feel all alone.
His strength shines bright, made perfect in our weakness,
For through our trials, our faith in Him is grown.

Chorus:

Count it all joy when God sends trials to grow you.
Trust in His power and never turn away.
No greater joy or glory doth await you—
The crown of life for what you choose today.

Chorus
—Doug Carragher and Stephanie Wesco - © 2020

During a phone call in September, Doug asked me if I had received his email from several weeks before with the words to a song he had begun to formulate. After I looked through my emails, I realized that I had in fact looked at it briefly but had not been able to fully process it at that point. That night, through smiles and tears, I revised what Doug had written and added a verse, and "Stephanie's Song (I Found My Savior True)" was completed. It was the summary of my past, present, and future by faith.

Stephanie's Song (I've Found My Savior True)

To Die Is Gain

We trusted Christ as Savior,
We made a plan for life.
We placed Him first in marriage;
He made me a preacher's wife.
Through years of faithful service,
We trusted in our God;
His Word a lamp unto our feet
To light each path we trod.
That horrible day came all too soon,
When we were torn apart.
One receiving his crown of glory,
And me a broken heart.
But I know our God was present there
In the midst of grief and pain,
As Christ, my Life, reminded me,
To die for Him, is gain.

Chorus:
We found our Savior worthy,
We proved our Savior true!
Though our plans were changed and altered,
We knew He would see us through.
Though His ways were not what we had planned,
We knew His way was best.
And our Savior said, "Come unto Me,
And I will give you rest."

The joy of the Lord is now my strength—
My focus on serving Him.
He is my Great Physician,
Making the pain grow dim.
Watching Him work His perfect plan
In all I daily do,
I have found my Savior worthy;
I've found my Savior true.

2nd Chorus:
I have found my Savior worthy,
I've proven my Savior true!
Though my plans have been changed and altered,
I know He will see me through.
Though His ways are not what I had planned,
I know His way is best.
And my Savior says, "Come unto Me,
And I will give you rest."

—*Doug Carragher and Stephanie Wesco - © 2020*

In the same period of weeks, the Lord took the poem I had written in January and turned it into a song. It is a conversation between my God and me, titled, "I Rest in Your Love."

I Rest In Your Love

My child, give Me your each expectation.
Wait on Me; My plan is best.
Come to Me; give Me your burdens.
Trust My love, and I'll give you rest.

Chorus:
Lord, here I am, take all my plans
And conform then to Your own.
This life's not mine; I'm bought with a price.
Take my heart and break up the stone.
Knowing You is worth all the pain;
Treasure laid up in Heaven is gain.
My life is Thine; I'm safe in Your hand.
Surrendered before You I stand.
I am Your child; I rest in Your love.

My ways are higher than you can imagine.

To Die Is Gain

Watch Me fulfill your heart's each desire.
Delight, My love, I never will leave you;
Though it's hot, I'm here in the fire.

I'm making you a vessel for service.
My one wish is to make you like Me.
Be transformed into My image;
A sacrifice I want you to be.

Chorus:

And one day, when you stand before Me
Clothed in My righteousness, glorified,
Then you will know that your pain was worth it.
Forever rest, content by My side.

> *Lord, here I am, take all my plans*
> *And conform then to Your own.*
> *This life's not mine; I'm bought with a price.*
> *Take my heart and break up the stone.*
> *Knowing You is worth all the pain;*
> *Treasure laid up in Heaven is gain.*
> *My life is Thine; I'm safe in Your hand.*
> *Surrendered before You I stand.*
> *I am Your child; I rest in Your love.*

—Stephanie Wesco - © 2020

Over the next couple of months, the Lord kept giving "songs in the night," as "Touch the Hem of His Garment" and "Serve Worthy, Christian Soldier" were written and music composed, after counseling sessions, phone calls with Doug and Debbie, and much time spent meditating on all God was doing in our hearts and lives.

Touch the Hem of His Garment

In a search for the healing, from my bleeding and pain,
In a crowd full of crying, from the hurting and lame,
My eyes searched for the Healer, Messiah, El-Shaddai.
I knew He could heal me through His love and His might.

Chorus
Touch the hem of His garment; see the love in His eyes.
A heart full of contrition, He will never despise.
Look to Christ for restoring of your heart, soul, and mind.
Touch the hem of His garment, where full healing you'll find.

My shameful affliction had been known by all.
I went to the Savior; at His feet I did fall.
I reached out, believing, touched the hem of His robe,
Through His power and healing, was made perfectly whole.

My life is restored now, and I'm finally free!
Gladly serving my Savior, who poured love on me.
You can find your full healing from your hurt and your pain.
Reach out and touch Him! Be never the same!

Chorus

—Doug Carragher and Stephanie Wesco - © 2020

Serve Worthy, Christian Soldier

A soldier serves his country with honor, dignity.
He prepares with great focus to defeat the enemy.
He moves mountains, walks through valleys, to fulfill his duty's call.
His standard firmly planted, a soldier cannot fall.
One's country is his castle, his pride, and his home.

He serves with obligation to ensure she's left alone.
Duty is his watchword and freedom his prize.
A soldier never runs; a soldier never hides.

Chorus
A Christian soldier serves his Lord with all of his might.
He hides within his heart Bible truths for the fight.
He never asks for trouble; he never seeks out pain.
He marches for his Savior, trusting Him alone for gain.
God will use him if he's willing to put aside his pride.
The foe already conquered for soldiers on God's side.
Serve, worthy Christian soldiers; be ready for the fight.
Your Leader is all-powerful! His ways are always right!

Our Captain is our fortress, our Savior, and might.
We serve because He's worthy, because He is our Light.
Be steadfast, my brethren, giving all to His fight.
Defeat is impossible and losing crucified!

Stand tall, my brethren; be ready for the fight!
You're serving your Glory, and victory is in sight!

Chorus

—Doug Carragher and Stephanie Wesco - © 2020

As our first real school year began, the Lord showed Himself so good to us through my youngest sister, who graciously agreed to be hired as a teacher/tutor for my children. Because of her daily diligence and encouragement in their lives, their progress in school has astounded me as they continue to make leaps and bounds forward in learning. I have a hard time processing the fact that my oldest son is now enrolled in our church's Bible Institute program and planning toward college, but it brings joy to my heart to see his desire to study, know and serve God more.

As the one-year anniversary of Charles' martyrdom loomed, I found myself dealing with many thoughts and emotions. I did not wish Charles back; I did not even ask why; I just hurt and did not want to have to remember all the horror and pain. The Lord knew I needed to be busy focusing on and pouring into others rather than thinking about myself. In His perfect timing, long beforehand, He had already lined up a perfect plan to keep me busy.

The children, Liberty, her younger sister, and I enjoyed a fun two-day-long road trip that ended in Louisiana, back at Southland Christian Camp. I had to marvel at all God had done in our hearts and lives since the last time we had been there. The first time we arrived at the camp, we were tired, traumatized, and seeking help and encouragement; the second time we arrived seeking to help and encourage others. It was my first opportunity to teach at a PTSD camp, and so much apprehension filled my heart. My feeling of helplessness left me begging God to do the work because I knew there was nothing in me that could. He answered, once again, with strength and grace. At the end of the week, I could do nothing but praise the Lord for the incredible ways He had worked in hearts and lives and had shown Himself strong. Because of Him, lives were impacted and changed, and hearts were helped and encouraged.

The kids at Southland Christian Camp in Ringgold, Louisiana

To Die Is Gain

As I looked back over the previous twelve months, all I could do was marvel at the multitude of ways God had worked. He truly had done exceedingly abundantly above all I could have asked or thought. He had brought so much beauty out of the terrible ashes, even though there were still many areas of ashes for which I hoped, desired and prayed He would bring beauty and new life. Had death really brought gain? Was the death of so many of my hopes and dreams, not to mention the martyrdom of the man I had loved, gain?

If God's perfect will had been accomplished in Charles' life and death; if souls were continuing to be saved; if Christ was being lifted up and glorified; if I knew Jesus more than I ever had before, then the answer is yes! To die to dreams, goals, plans, and ambitions in order for my life to be Christ and to be walking the perfect path He had chosen for my life, then indeed, to die is gain. God clearly held my past and holds my present and future, and that makes living for Him exciting.

Our last family picture with Charles

APPENDIX A: CHARLES' SERMON NOTES

"How to Have an Effective Ministry Reaching Others and How to Truly Experience the Promise of White Harvest Fields (John 4:1–43)"

Be Spirit-filled and don't miss divine appointments. Look for that "person of peace."

1. (v 4, 7) "must needs go through . . . there cometh a woman of Samaria to draw water"
2. Luke 10: Look for that person of peace. Many would have discounted her as riffraff; God made her into a trophy of His grace and a messenger of peace.

Be Prepared.

1. Be ready to sacrifice and "die to self."
2. (v 6, 32) "being wearied with His journey…I have food to eat that ye know not of." Forego our own "comfort zones" and sacrifice some of our own privacy and comfort.
3. Kernel of corn that falls into ground and dies (illustration)

Go Anywhere.

1. The gospel has no prejudices, and neither should you in selecting to whom you will deliver the gospel message.
2. Jesus has promised Himself to light the path of every man that comes into the world (1:9).
3. (v 9) "How is it ... of me ... who am a woman ... of Samaria." History of Samaritans in past and present. We shall soon hear her history, which was quite dirty.

Share Christ Creatively.

1. Communicate creatively the hope of Christ and the gospel.
2. (v 10) "If thou knewest the Gift of God ... who it was ... I would have given thee living water." Basic principle of Christian counseling is to always give the hope of God! When evangelizing, always give hope to the unbeliever, concerning the power of God to change their life and to quench their thirst!
3. The prophets of the OT were very creative. Jesus was as well (parables). They put many hours into dreaming up graphic ways of presenting God's message to God's people. The OT Scriptures are considered even by unsaved literary experts to be some of the best literature every penned.

Be Loving.

1. Be loving, but confrontational, with the truth and about sin. Don't let smokescreens distract you.
2. (v 12) "Art thou greater ..." I have visited this very well (Jacob's Well, 175' deep, deepest in Israel). Many religions today, including in Africa, hold onto relics instead of the

truth! Jesus is greater and more personal than their false religions of works!
3. (v 17) "I have no husband." Jesus took her to task and did not [accept] her purposefully vague and deceitful statements. She was a harlot who had been married to five different men, and thus, the man she now had was a whoremonger!
4. (v. 16–18) "Thou hast had five husbands . . . and he whom . . . ." Don't sidestep the sin of the sinner. Illustration: Go fishing with a net, not a hook. "What you win them with is what you win them to."
5. (v 19–20, 21–24, 26) "Our fathers worshipped in this mountain . . . ye worship ye know not what." The woman tried to divert Jesus to a side conversation and away from the truth about her, which hurt! Jesus was not a "rationalist" or even a semi-rationalist but a pre-suppositionalist! (Explain Mount Gerizim and their Torah law). Show unsaved folks how much greater God is than anything they have! This is hope-giving and convicting all at the same time!
6. v. 14, 25–26 "I know that Messiah cometh . . ." What do you know? Jesus was so patient with her, and she *finally* saw the Light! Jesus was there to meet her need! What amazing timing! What amazing timing it was in my life when I first saw Christ, and He showed me the glorious light of the good news of the gospel!

For the unbeliever, Jesus is a spring of water springing up into everlasting life! Have you ever drunk of this living and life-giving water that Jesus offered this woman, in place of her diseased life of sin and shame? Or do you insist on rather trying to live on the dirty, disease-ridden water of this world?

For the believer who continues even as he received Christ Jesus to walk in Him, the Holy Spirit continues to flow out of His belly! "He that believeth on me, as the Scripture hath said, out of his belly (innermost being) shall flow rivers of living water." (Holy Spirit) We have in us the same power of Jesus to offer and demonstrate this same living water through Christ in us!

My wife and I and our family have been called by the Lord of the Harvest to the ripe harvest fields of Cameroon, West Africa. We "must needs go" to Cameroon. There the harvest is great! It is the Lord of the Harvest who leads us each to our location of service. Let's not miss our calling! What is your calling? Are you missing it because you are not willing to go through your Samaria, to which God has led you?

As one song puts it, "How can we reach a world we never touch?" Jesus had no patience or time for the hypocritical Pharisee believers of His day, yet He would regularly eat and carefully reach out to winebibbers and sinners of all sorts. We see Mary the harlot, Simon, Zacchaeus, and so many others who Jesus had compassion on, seeing them as sheep, having no Shepherd. Jesus came to "seek and to save the lost."

Before He ascended to the right hand of His Father in heaven, He promised to give us all His authority and power as well as the filling of His Holy Spirit. He then issued the Great Commission to us as the church. There are so many good things a church can do, but we must never forget why Jesus said He had left us here! Each generation is here to reach their entire generation around the world with the gospel of Jesus Christ, just like the apostles did by the grace of God in their generation, which was turned upside down for the truth!

Sermon: Living for Eternity

Basic Outline; Matthew 19–20

(Charles had heard another missionary preach a message using this outline before we started deputation, but it very quickly became his own—in more ways than one!)

1. Living for eternity is better than living for the present.
2. Leaving the choice of reward in the Lord's hands is far wiser than choosing for yourself.

Appendix A: Charles' Sermon Notes

3. *How* you finish is more important than *when* you begin!
4. Serving Christ always comes with a cost.
5. Christ is looking for people to serve in His vineyard.
6. The currency in the Kingdom will be what? Service to the King and His Kingdom!

APPENDIX B: CHARLES' QUOTES

"The currency of heaven is going to be quite different from the currency of this world."

"Living for eternity is better than living for the present."

"It's more important for us to focus on suffering and persecution than on the reward."

"He tells Peter later on, 'Are you ready to share in my sufferings? Are you really ready to drink my cup?' And Jesus would ask that tonight. Jesus would say, 'Don't focus on the reward; focus on taking up the cross and following me!' Focus on the cross, not the reward."

"Living for eternity is worth it."

"You will never regret living for eternity."

"Faith is putting your energies into something you cannot see or touch or hold."

Appendix B: Charles' Quotes

"We need to figure out what makes eternity tick and live for that."

"How you finish is more important than when you began."

"God cares more about how you finish the race than when you began."

"Finish going out strong and faithful in His power and grace, and you'll never regret it."

"How you finish is very important."

"There are a lot of things people in America are living for, and I hate to say it, but a lot of the Christian world is not living for eternity."

"I think it's healthy for every young man or woman, before you go into whatever career you think God has for you, to take a short-term trip to some place like South Africa or Cameroon. To see and give God a chance to work in your life—to let your eyes influence your heart."

"Living for eternity is worth it, but many times we are in the background looking at the wealth and we're weighing this all out and we're doing like Peter saying, 'God if I do this, what will I get for it?'"

"One day King Jesus will be on the throne. And when King Jesus is on the throne, the tables will turn quite drastically. The currency will be amazingly different than the US dollar that runs the world now. The currency in the kingdom will be so different you will look back at this kingdom and say, 'How did I miss it?'"

Appendix B: Charles' Quotes

"Jesus says, 'Look, it's going to be good. It's going to be a hundredfold, but leave the choice with Me!' Let Him decide your hire. Whether you're forty years old when you get saved or whether you're ten years old, you just go to work and be faithful."

"I know the Lord has talked about rewards that are in heaven, and I know He means for us to understand those things, but right now—the here and now is to focus on being a good soldier who 'bears under' like 2 Timothy 2 talks about—who gives all not to be entangled with the affairs of this life, who preaches the word in season and out of season, reproves, rebukes, exhorts with all longsuffering and doctrine, who's alert to the itching ears, who goes out as a good soldier of Jesus Christ."

"God cares about faithfulness and good stewards."

"What happened to the "on fire for God"? What happened to the 'Where's my cross; I'll take it and follow you today, Jesus?' What happened to that focus?"

"Some of you may have started out well. You used to go soul winning. You used to spend serious time in prayer. You used to avoid worldly attractions. The love of Christ constrained you.... You walked in the light and tried to grow for the Lord.... Maybe you used to be that way and you've fallen away from the Lord. Now you need to realize that how you finish is important—it's very important."

"I believe in eternal security. And I believe you're saved once you're saved, but sometimes we forget to preach there's

Appendix B: Charles' Quotes

more to it than that. There's such a thing as the bema seat of Christ. And we will receive the things done, in our glorified bodies, according to our works. And some glorified bodies will shine like the sun or the moon and other will shine like Betelgeuse (like the great stars in heaven). And those crowns represent things done in our bodies. And of course, we know it's all by God's grace and we cast that all back at His feet. But there are going to be Christians who are cleaning toilets in eternity and there are going to be Christians who are ruling over ten cities. . . . It's going to work out that way. In fact, those who suffer with Christ are going to really be reigning!"

"Serving Christ always comes with a cost. And if you're not ready for that, get your act together and go back to your prayer closet. This world is not our home. We are called 'sojourners' and 'pilgrims' and 'soldiers,' not people who make big homesteads and focus on living in this world."

"All the things of this world that we live for are going to be dissolved; they're going to melt; they're going to atomically disintegrate. There will be no fancy car. There will be no nice boat. There will be no big glamorous home. It will all be gone! Every lick of it. So, we'd better figure out how to live for eternity. 'Seeing then that all these things shall be dissolved,' Peter goes on to say, 'what manner of persons ought ye to be in all holy living and godliness, looking for and hasting unto the coming of the day of God'" (2 Peter 3:11–12).

"We're like the rich young ruler sometimes. We want to figure out some way to make a side hobby out of Christianity. We want to figure out a way (without the cost, without losing any of earth's treasures) to still *have a comfortable life and still lay-up treasure in heaven. How foolish! How utterly foolish that is to trade off heaven's treasures!"*

"I'm all for family. I came from a big family; my wife came from a big family. But we're not here to set up towers of Babel. We can have so many things in a family that can be business, that can be ministry, that can be church, that our young people aren't willing to stretch out their necks and go out into the world and preach the gospel to every creature across the world."

"We need to realize that serving Christ always comes with a cost."

"If you don't sacrifice much for Christ, you're not storing up treasure in heaven."

"If you don't stand up to it, this world's system will come up with a way to keep you too busy to serve Jesus. There is nothing wrong with work, but I know many men who work too much. Some people today are just 'clever' enough to work themselves out of a whole bunch of eternal rewards. I don't call that clever; I call that foolish."

"Don't be so short-sighted that you miss the fact that God is testing you with 'things' to see if you will trust Him enough to sacrifice."

"If you really want to know (as a father) the heart of a young man coming to court your daughter, ask to see his finances. Ask to see his checkbook and see where he spends his money. Learn about how he spends his

money because where a man's treasure is—that's where his heart is."

"Serving Christ comes with a sacrifice, young men."

"Christ is looking for people to serve in His vineyard. Let's not miss how simple this is. Because many times people say, 'I don't know if God wants me' or 'I don't know if God can use me.' Hey, look, the problem is that the harvest is huge! The fields are white everywhere, and there's not enough help! There's not enough help in Cameroon! There's not enough help . . . in Kenya! There not enough help . . . in South Africa! There is not enough help anywhere you go! And sometimes we forget how simple it is while we stand around waiting on God to strike us with a bolt of lightning. But there's lots and lots of reaping and sowing all over the vineyard ready to happen!"

"[Jesus] doesn't care if it's the eleventh hour and you don't play the violin or harmonica or piano or do chalk talks. He made you who you are, and He has a purpose for you. He's looking for people to work in His vineyard. Are you ready to work?"

"If you are going to live for eternity, the goal is to find out how many people you can serve. That's what makes greatness in God's kingdom."

"Lord, we need you to help us not to see so darkly, but through your Holy Spirit to help us catch a little bit of a glimpse of the heavenly city where the streets are gold, and the gates are made of pearls, and Jesus sits on the throne with hands that have been pierced, Lord, Who

Appendix B: Charles' Quotes

humbled Himself and became obedient unto death, even the death of the cross, that at the name of Jesus, one day, every knee shall bow. And Lord, I want to bow the knee, having done through your grace what I could. I don't want to end up with a handful of [worthless money]. Lord, I want to lay up treasures in heaven where moth and rust cannot destroy and where thieves cannot break through and steal. I understand, Lord, that where my treasure is my heart is. We came into this world naked and we shall go out naked. The love of money and shiny things is the root of all evil."

"Lord, I pray you'd touch my life and my children's lives. Lord, I don't want them to see a hypocrite in a father. I want them to see a man who wants them to excel and surpass the servant opportunities you've given me to serve you even more."

"Lord, we just pray that You would help us to grow in the grace and in the knowledge of our Lord and Savior Jesus Christ so we can glorify You more. Help us to forget those things which are behind and to press toward the mark of the prize of the high calling of God in Christ Jesus. May You be glorified through it all, Lord. We know it's only by Your empowerment and Your grace, and we look forward to the day in heaven when we can cast our crowns (and those things done in our bodies according to our works), to cast them all before Your throne and tell You, Lord, how You're worthy to receive all the glory, and all the honor, and all the power, and all the thanksgiving, and to thank You, Lord, for creating us for Your pleasure."

"We do have a very caring and loving God to lean upon (be

it here or in the U.S.A.), who is beyond doubt in sovereign control of who falls and where and to what weapons—even down to the small sparrow. [from an email sent to friends and family in the States, dated Sunday, October 21, 2018, nine days before his martyrdom]."

APPENDIX C: CHARLES' SPIRITUAL PREPARATION

SPIRITUAL PREPARATIONS FOR YOUR LIFE

To experience the best this "life" has to offer you must be spiritually prepared. The essential requirement of this journey is to know Jesus as your Lord and Savior so He can be your Guide. If you have never received Him, or if you're not sure, there are four things you must understand and accept:

- **Recognize that you need a Savior**
- The greatest question in the Bible is How do you find Christ? The first step in finding Christ is to recognize that you need him, that you are a sinner, that you have violated the principles of truth in the word of God. The Bible says *"For all have sinned, and come short of the glory of God"* ~Romans 3:23 I have sinned and you have sinned, and because we have sinned, we must have the blood of Jesus Christ cleanse us from all sin. Our morality cannot save us, our goodness cannot save us, and our acts of kindness cannot save us. Only Jesus Christ can save us.

- **Repent and Confess your sin**

Appendix C: Charles' Spiritual Preparation

- The Bible says in *"If we confess our sins, he is faithful and just to forgive us our sins, and to cleanse us from all unrighteousness."* ~1 John 1:9 Now you might be thinking that you are not good enough. I want you to know that God can save anyone. It does not matter what you have done, He can and will save you. God loves us even though we are sinners. The Bible says in *"But God commendeth his love toward us, in that, while we were yet sinners, Christ died for us."* ~Romans 5:8 God has made it possible through the gift of his son for you to be saved. That provision is God's gift. The Bible says in *"For the wages of sin is death; but the gift of God is eternal life through Jesus Christ our Lord."* ~Romans 6:23 For it is by Grace that you have been saved through Faith. It is not of yourself; it is the gift of God that you have been saved, not by works so that no one can boast. So you see, you cannot get to Heaven by being good or by doing his works or acts of kindness. You only get to Heaven because you have confessed your sins. There must be the repentance of sin, which means you must turn away from your sins. The Bible says in Mark 1:15 *"the kingdom of God is at hand: repent ye, and believe the gospel."*

Definitions:

- Repent means to turn away, walk and go another way.
- The Gospel - The life, death and resurrection of Jesus Christ.
- "That if you confess with your mouth to our Lord Jesus and if you believe in your heart, that God raised Jesus from the dead, you will be saved. For it is with your heart that you believe and are justified and with your mouth that you confess your sin and are saved." ~Romans 5:8 The result is eternal salvation, for the Bible says in Romans 10:13 *"For whosoever shall call upon the name of the Lord shall be saved."* ~Roman 10:13

- The Bible says that salvation is found in no other name given among men under Heaven, other than the name of our Lord Jesus Christ. So, if you want to find Christ all you have to do is pray this prayer. But the words themselves will not save you. Only faith in Jesus Christ can provide salvation!

- **<u>A Sinner's Prayer for Eternal Salvation</u>**
- **What is the sinner's prayer?**
- The sinner's prayer is a Christian term for a prayer that is said when someone wants to repent of their sin, ask God for forgiveness and state belief in the life, death, and saving resurrection of Jesus Christ. Romans 10:9-10, says "That if thou shalt confess with thy mouth the Lord Jesus, and shalt believe in thine heart that God hath raised him from the dead, thou shalt be."
- Millions have come to a saving relationship with Jesus Christ through church services, friends, and family leading them in a salvation prayer. However, it is not words in a prayer that save. Jesus Christ alone has the power to save through faith. Understanding that it's not the prayer that saves, it's the repentance and faith behind the prayer that lays hold of salvation.
- **Example of a sinner's prayer (While meaning it in your heart say a prayer like this):**
- Lord Jesus Christ, I confess that I'm a sinner. I ask you to forgive me of my sins and to cleanse me of all unrighteousness. I believe that Your Son Jesus died in my place, to pay the penalty for my sin, and rose again for my salvation. I want to turn from my sinful ways, so I now ask you, Lord Jesus, to come into my life as my Savior and my Lord. I will serve you and obey you. I will read your word and I will follow Christ from this day forward all the days of my life. In Jesus name I pray, Amen.

Appendix C: Charles' Spiritual Preparation

- Now with your faith in Jesus Christ you have stepped from darkness into the light.
- The difficulties of living as a Christian in a sinful world are many. Therefore, it is important that you seek other Christians to help you sustain your resolve. Go to Church as often as you can to help you support your beliefs. Please ask the person leading this seminar to recommend a pastor and local church. It is the Lord's will for your journey.
- If you have prayed this prayer in sincere faith, you may want to put your initials by the prayer along with today's date as a reminder that you have come to Christ in faith, trusting him as your Lord and Savior.

Used by permission Doug Carragher

Made in the USA
Monee, IL
10 October 2020